ESSENTIAL ELEMENTS for Strings

COMPREHENSIVE STRING METHOD

MICHAEL ALLEN • ROBERT GILLESPIE • PAMELA TELLEJOHN HAYES
ARRANGEMENTS BY JOHN HIGGINS

These piano accompaniments can provide helpful guidance for teaching beginning string players. The format includes a cue line to provide the teacher or pianist with a visual guide of the student melody part.

The accompaniments have been arranged to match the style and harmony of the accompaniments available online. These tracks are available online using the code included with student books and the teacher manual. They may be used for teaching or performance and offer a variety of styles, from classical to contemporary popular music. You may want to alter these piano accompaniments to meet your specific needs. Chord symbols are provided.

ISBN 979-835013661-6

D MAJOR

1. TUNING TRACK

2. D MAJOR SCALE – Round *(When group A reaches ②, group B begins at ①)*

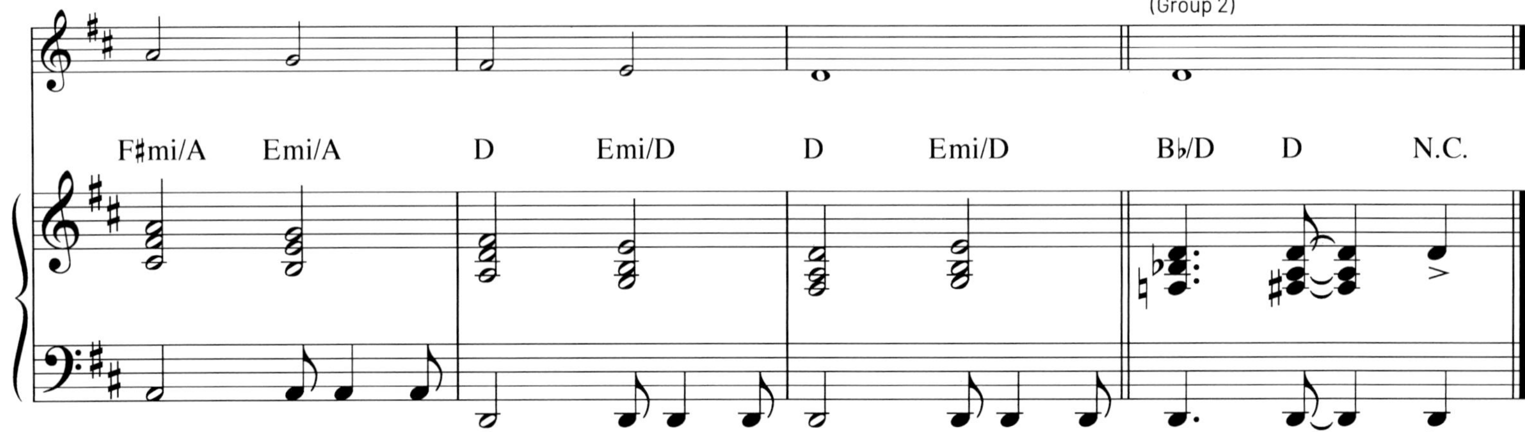

3. D MAJOR ARPEGGIO

4. D MAJOR MANIA

D MAJOR

D/A
F♯7
G
E7
A7
G7
D7
5. THEME FROM LONDON SYMPHONY
Franz J. Haydn (1732–1809)
legato
D
A7/D
D
A/C♯
D6
D
G/B
F♯mi/A
Emi/G
D/F♯
Emi7
G
D/A
A
D
A7/D
D
A/C♯
D6
D
Bmi
A/C♯
G/B
A/G G
D/A
A7
D

6. D MAJOR IN THREES

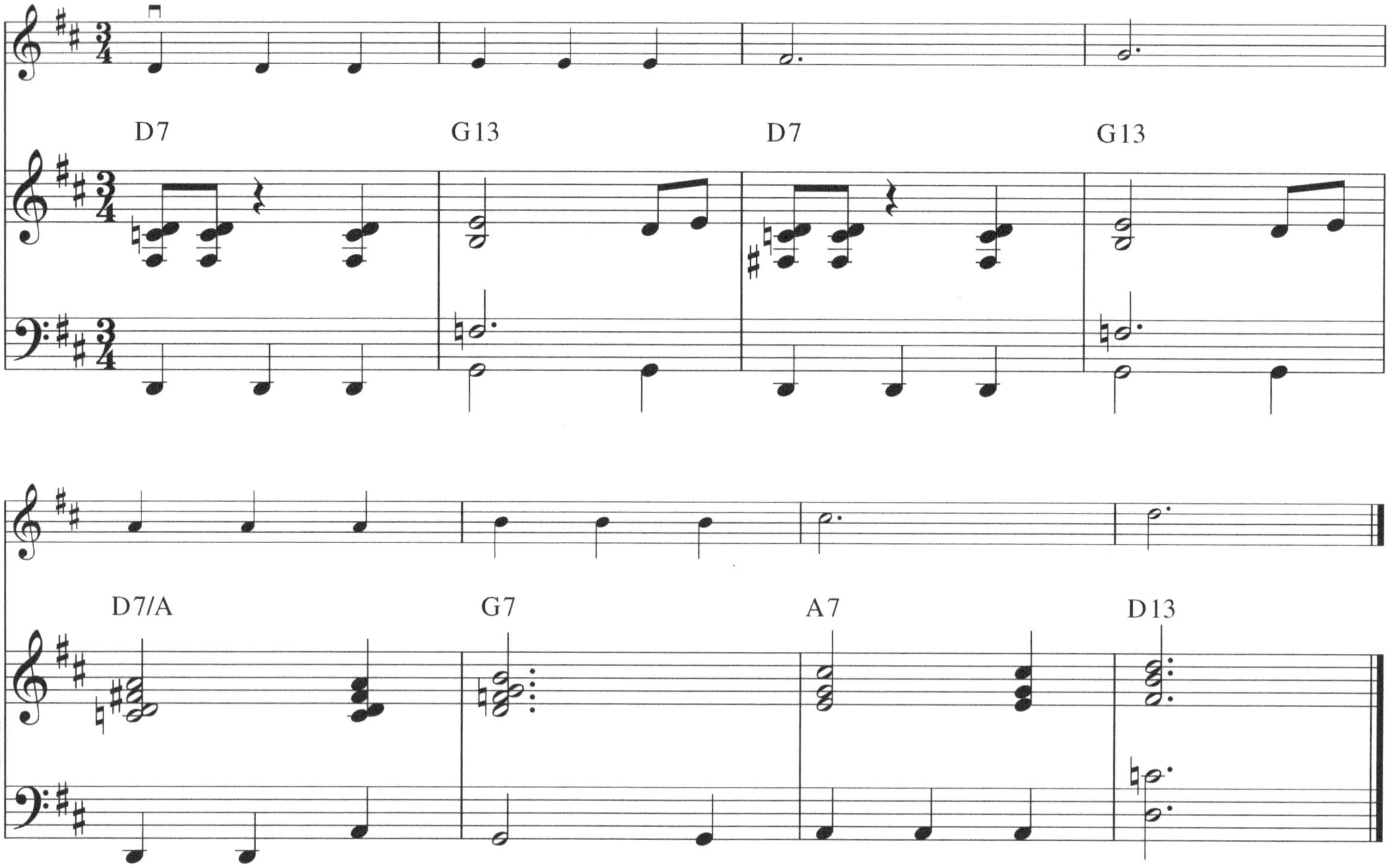
D7
G13
D7
G13
D7/A
G7
A7
D13

7. DYNAMIC CONTRASTS

f
p
D
A/D
G/B
F♯mi/A
f
p
f
G/A
A/G
Gmi7
G/A
D
f

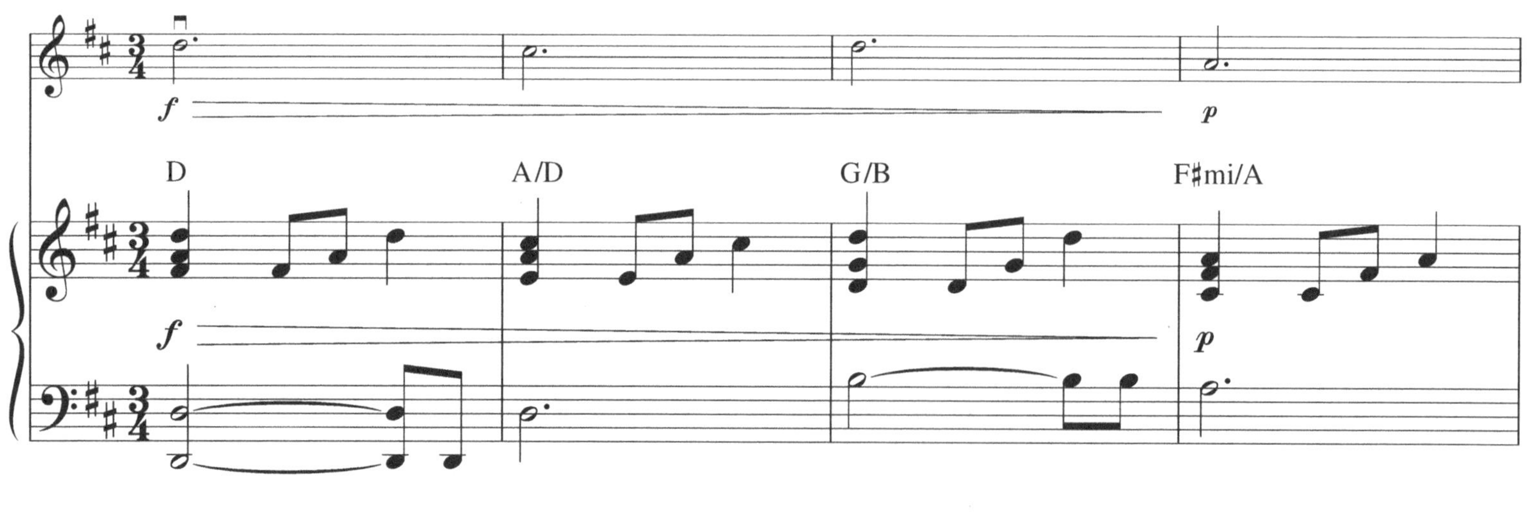

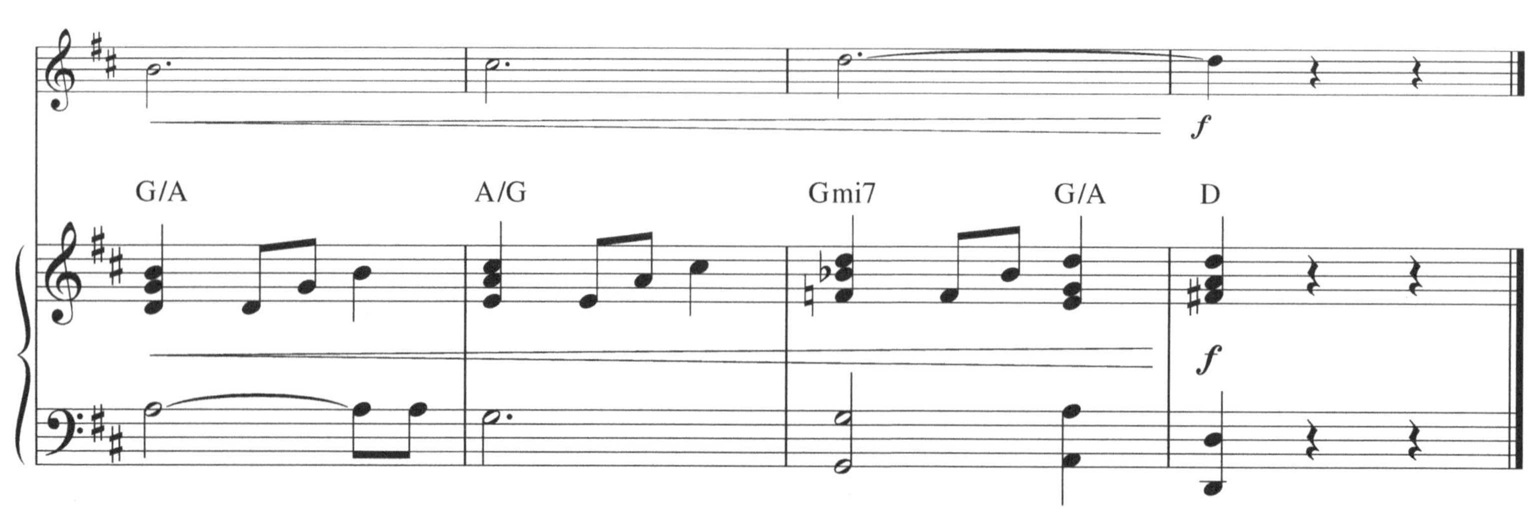

8. MORNING (from Peer Gynt)

Edvard Grieg (1843–1907)

9. BARCAROLLE

Jacques Offenbach (1819–1880)

G MAJOR

10. G MAJOR SCALE – Round

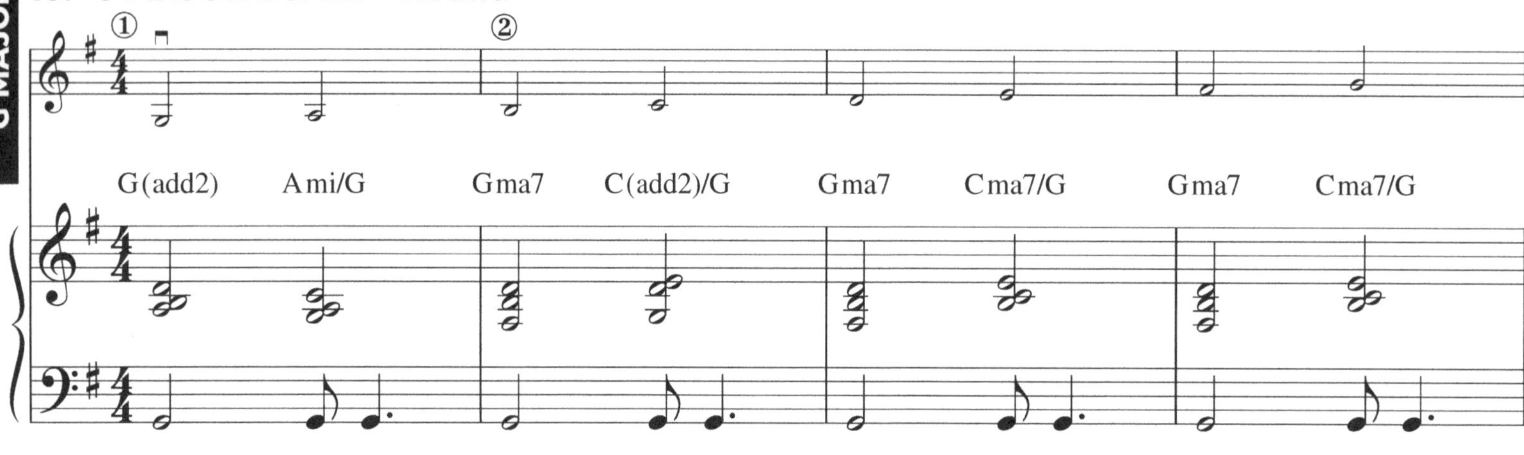

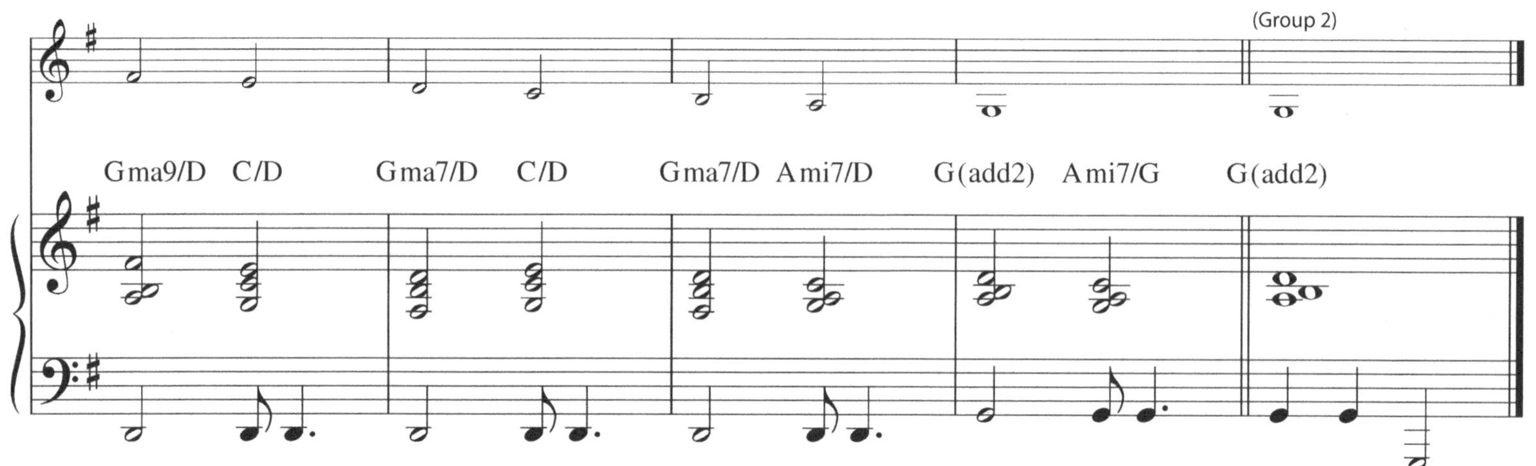

11. G MAJOR ARPEGGIO

12. SCALE INTERVALS

13. CHESTER

William Billings (1746–1800)

G MAJOR

14. G MAJOR SCALE

15. G MAJOR ARPEGGIO

16. INTONATION ENCOUNTER – Duet

17. THE OUTBACK

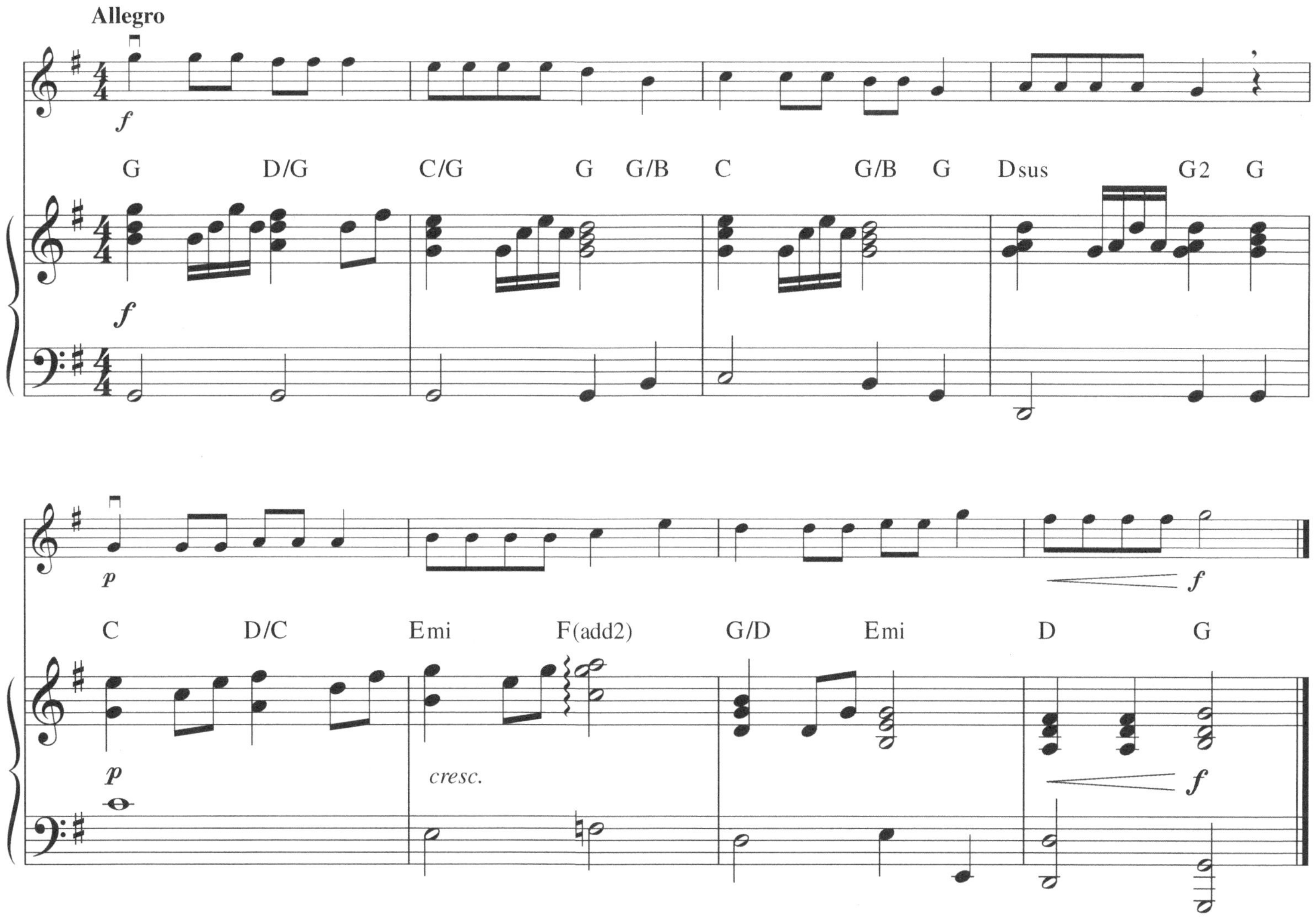

Allegro

f

G D/G C/G G G/B C G/B G Dsus G2 G

f

p

C D/C Emi F(add2) G/D Emi D G

p *cresc.* *f*

18. C MAJOR SCALE

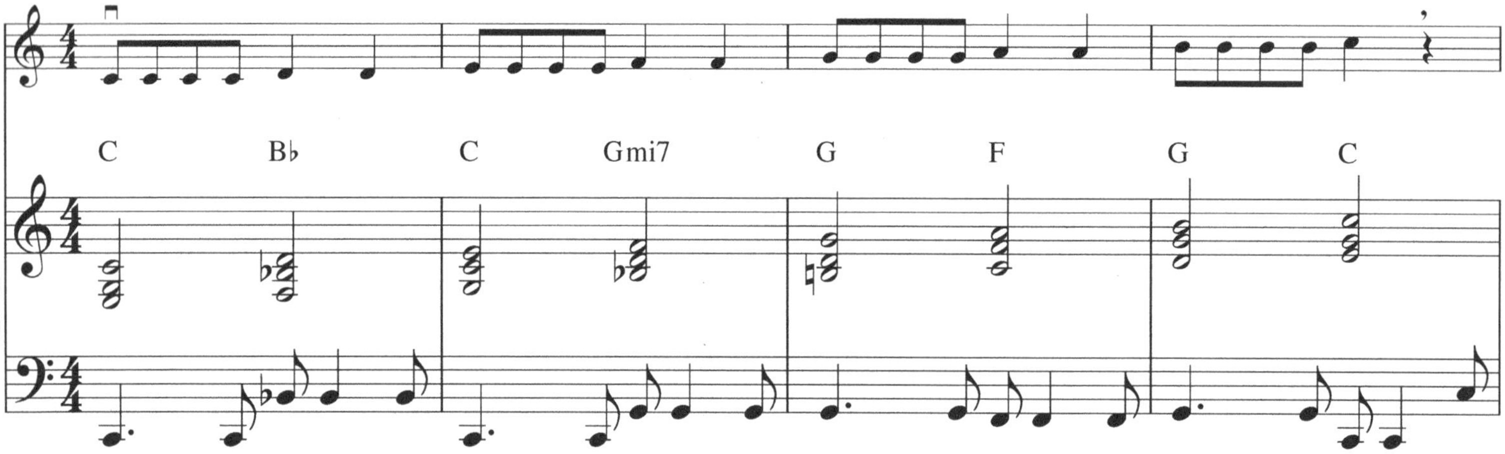
C Bb C Gmi7 G F G C

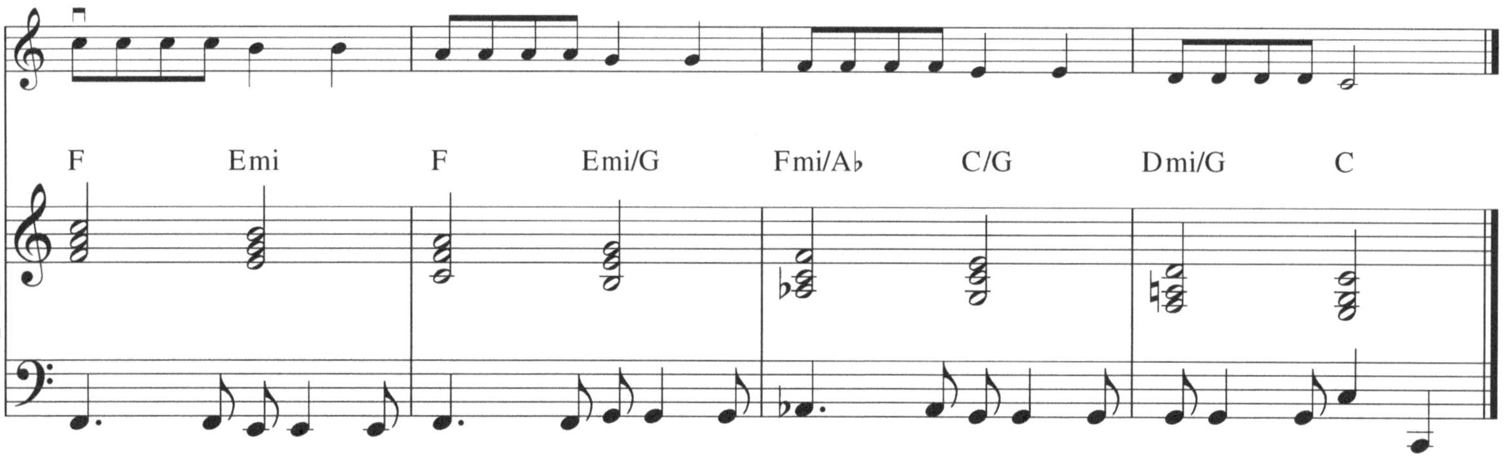
F Emi F Emi/G Fmi/Ab C/G Dmi/G C

19. C MAJOR ARPEGGIO

F C G C G C G C

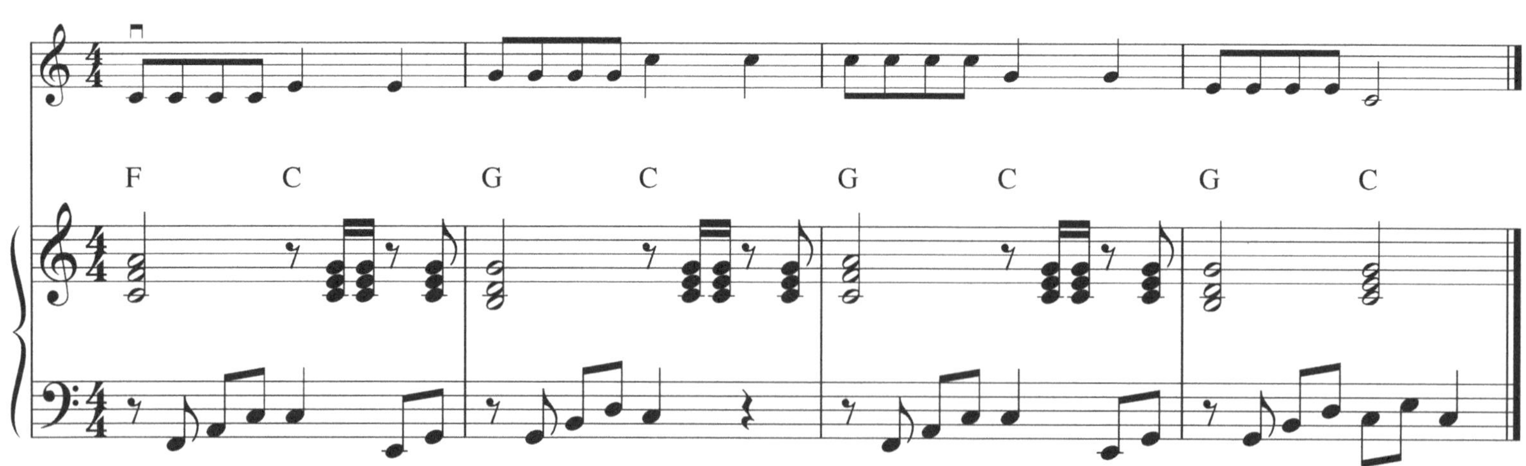

20. C MAJOR DUET

21. BINGO

22. C MAJOR SCALE – Round

23. C MAJOR ARPEGGIO

24. C MAJOR MANIA

25. CROSSROADS

26. THE DOT ALWAYS COUNTS
Student books have repeats after 4 bars.
Dma7
Gma7
Emi7
A7
Bmi7
B♭9
F♯mi7
F9(♯11)
Emi7
A7
B♭/E♭
D
RHYTHMS
27. ALOUETTE
Allegretto
French Folk Song
mf
D13
G13
D7
A7
D13
G9
C13
D13
G13
D7
A7
G9
C7
C♯7
D7

28. RIGAUDON

Henry Purcell (1659–1695)

29. ESSENTIAL CREATIVITY – CANDY MOUNTAIN ROCK

RHYTHMS

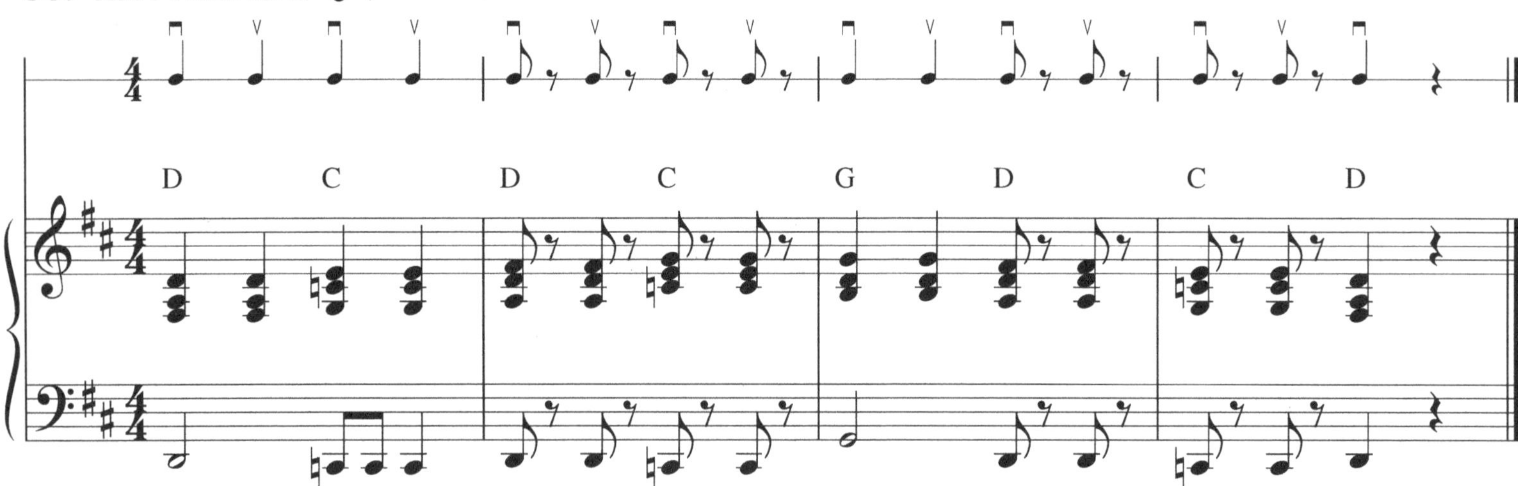

31. EIGHTH NOTES ON THE BEAT

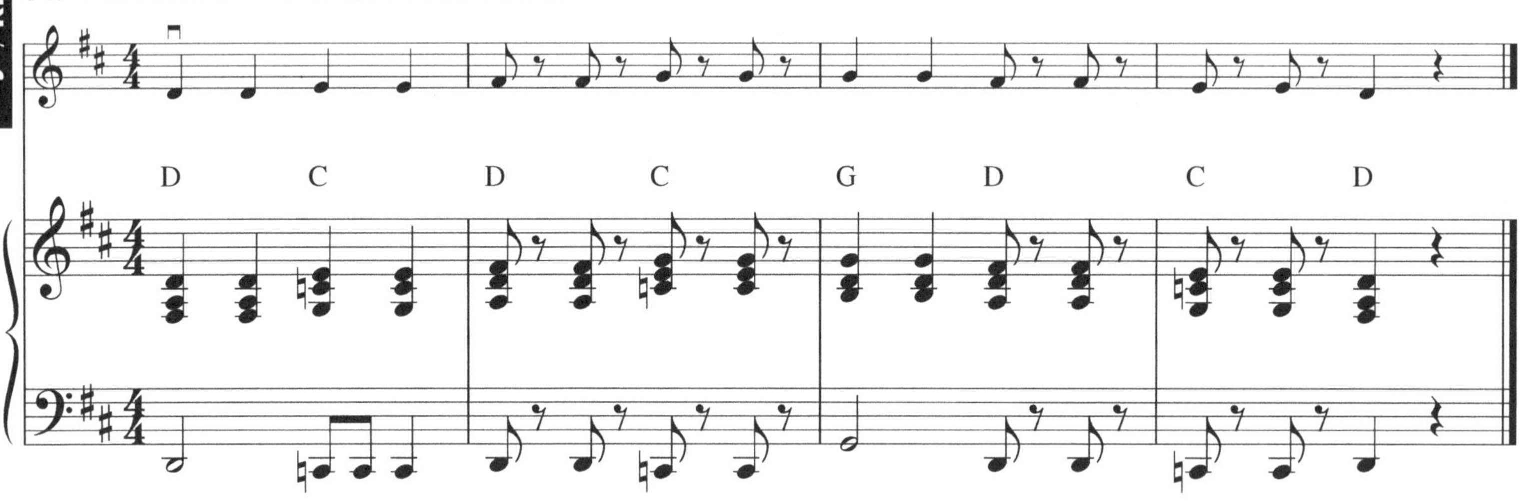

32. SHORT AND SWEET

Student books have repeats, not 1st and 2nd endings.

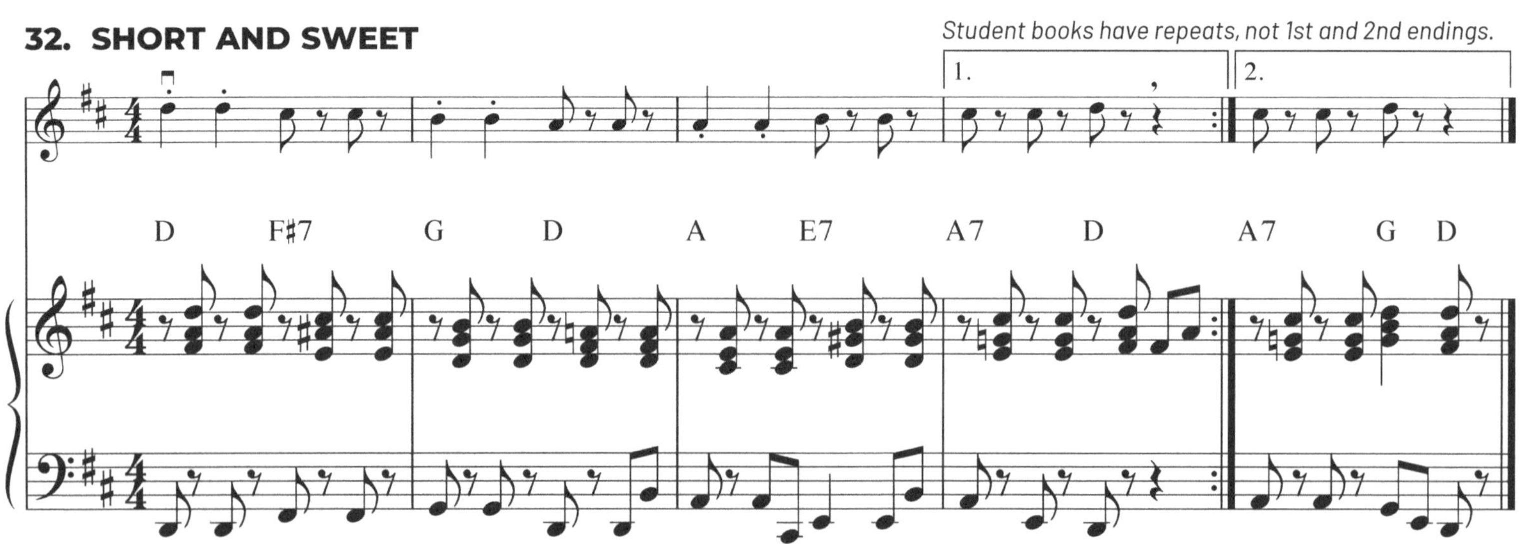

RHYTHMS

33. RHYTHM RAP

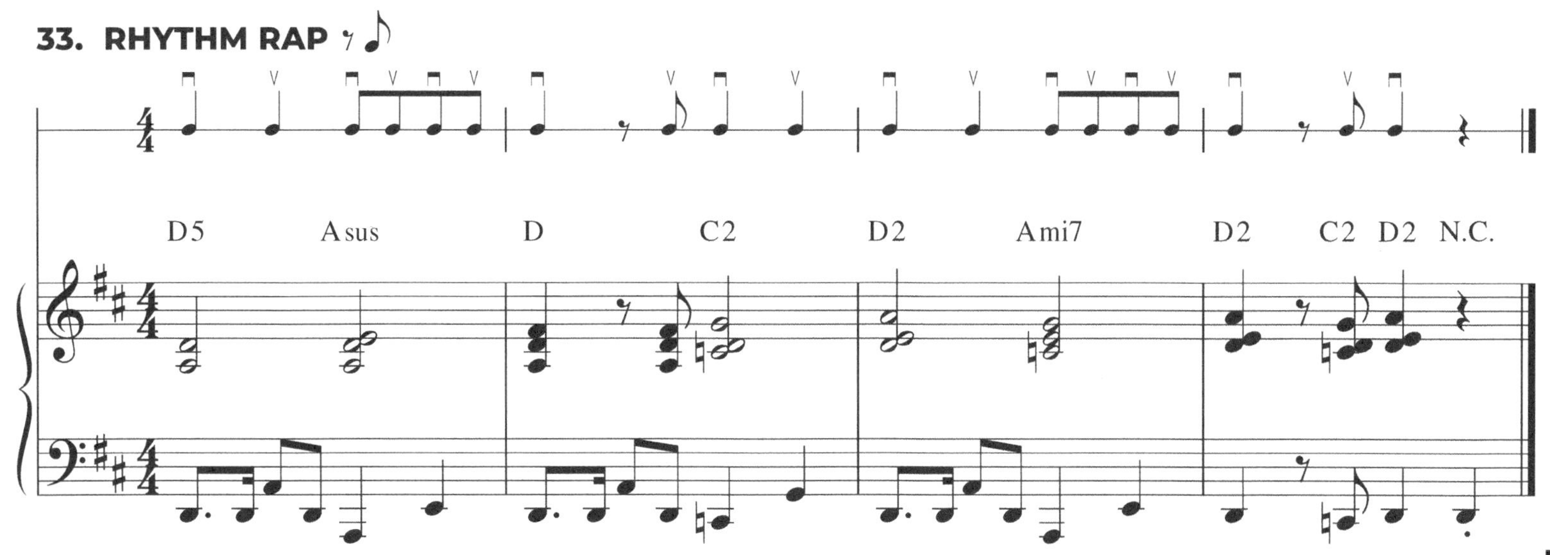

34. EIGHTH NOTES OFF THE BEAT

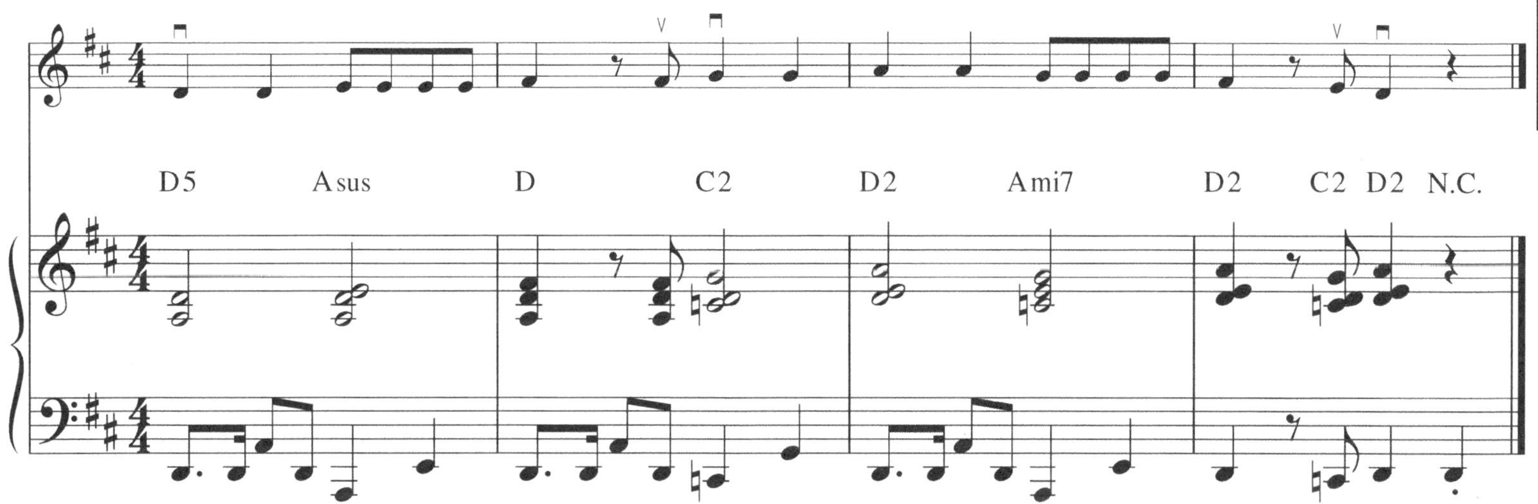

35. SUNNY DAY

36. ESSENTIAL ELEMENTS QUIZ – JESSE JAMES

Folk Ballad from Missouri

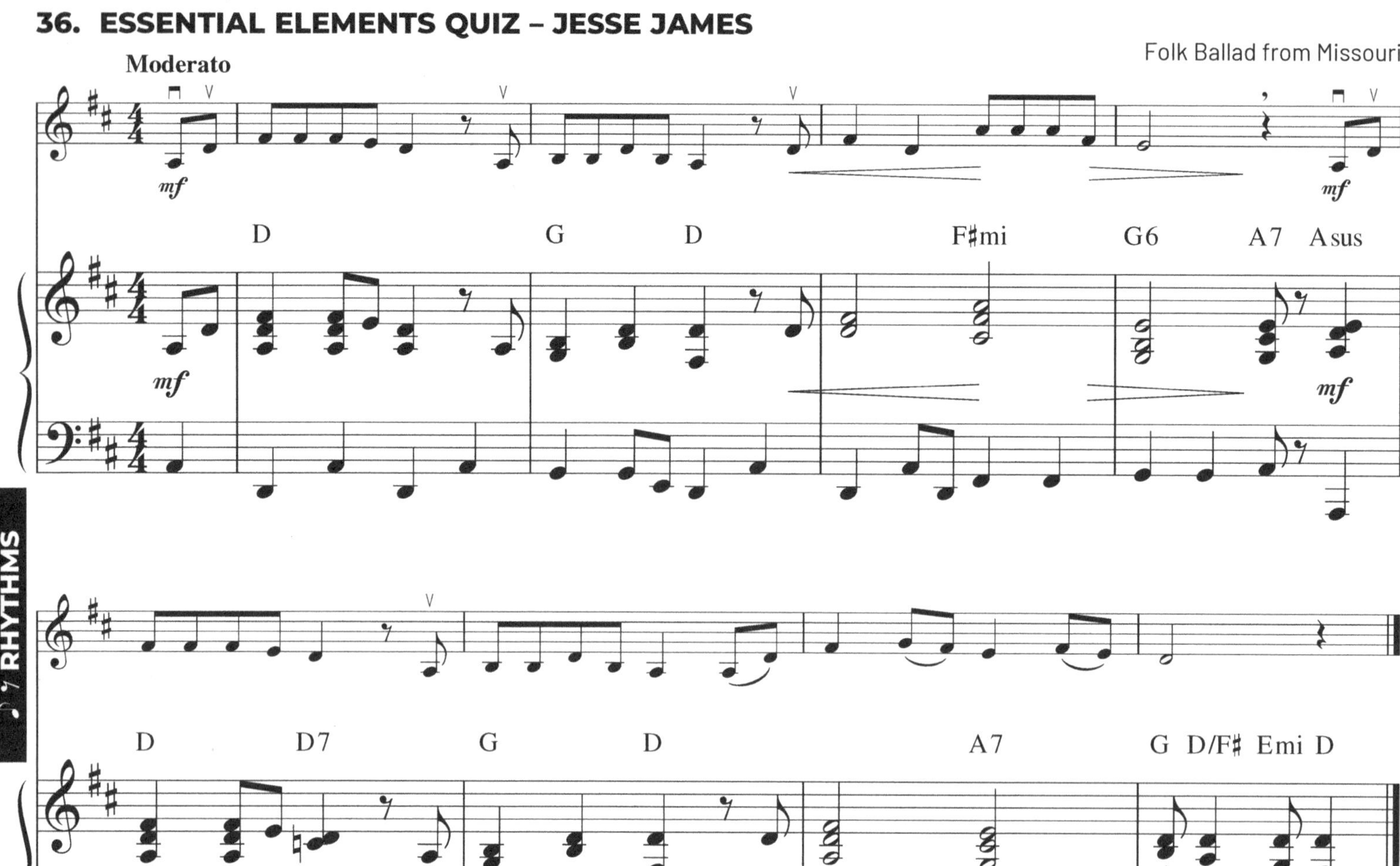

37. RHYTHM RAP

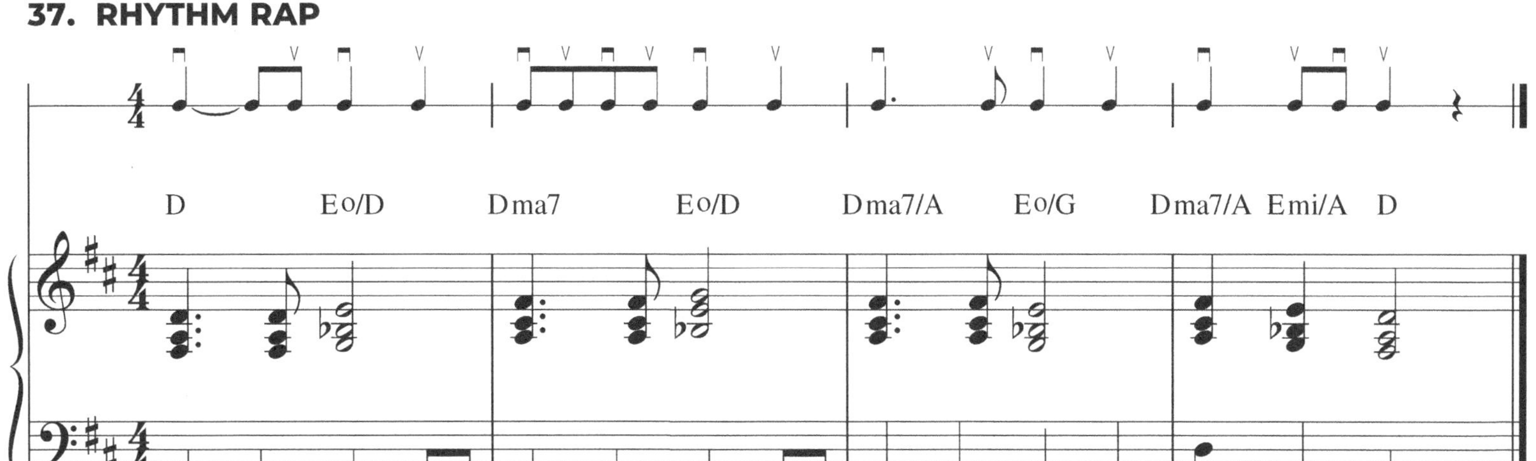

38. THE DOT COUNTS

RHYTHMS

39. WATCH THE DOT

Student books have repeats, not 1st and 2nd endings.

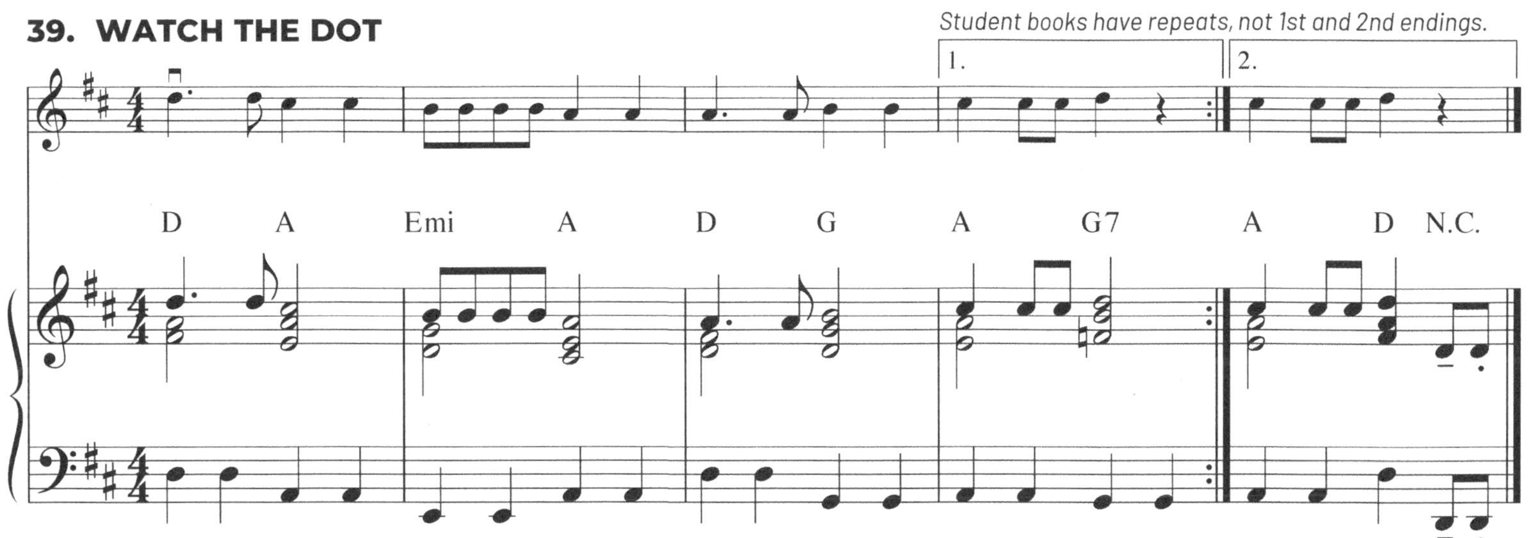

40. D MAJOR SEQUENCE

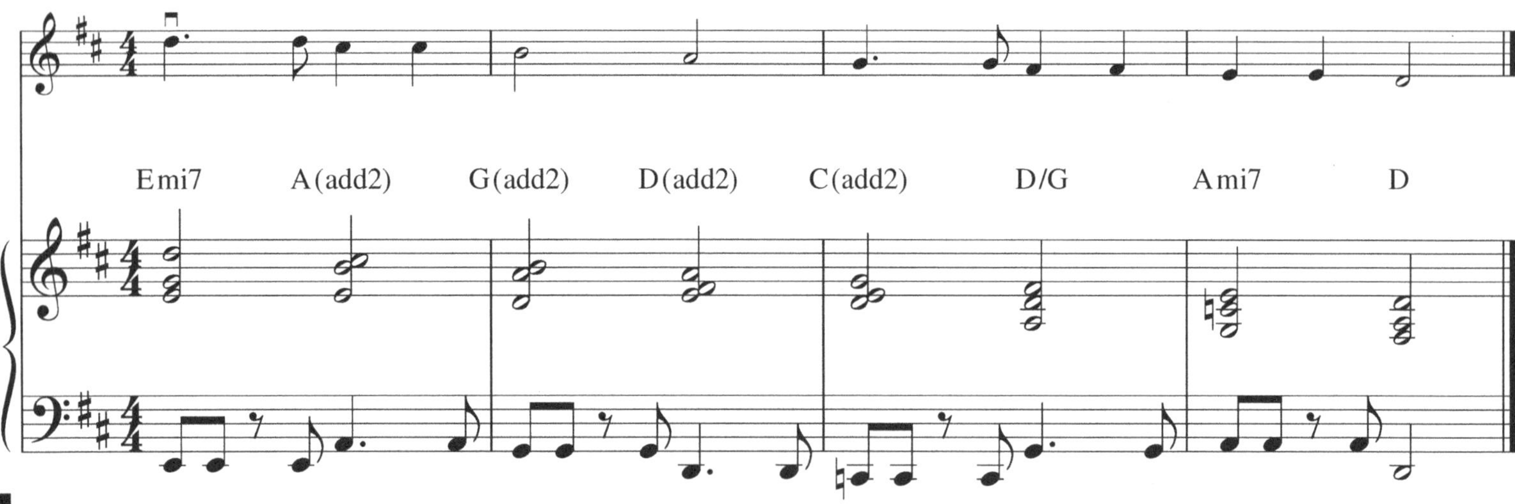

41. DOTS ON THE MOVE

42. D MAJOR BONANZA – Duet

43. A CAPITAL SHIP

46. THEME FROM NEW WORLD SYMPHONY
Lento
Antonin Dvorák (1841–1904)
D
A7/D
A G/B A/C♯
RHYTHMS
D
F♯+ Bo
Emi/G A
D
rit.
47. ESSENTIAL ELEMENTS QUIZ – RONDEAU
Andantino
Jean-Joseph Mouret (1682–1738)
D A D
G/D D
Emi7 D/F♯
F♯/A G/B
A/C♯ Emi/B
A
1.
2.
A
D
rit.

SHARP KEYS

48. LET'S READ "C♯" (C-sharp)

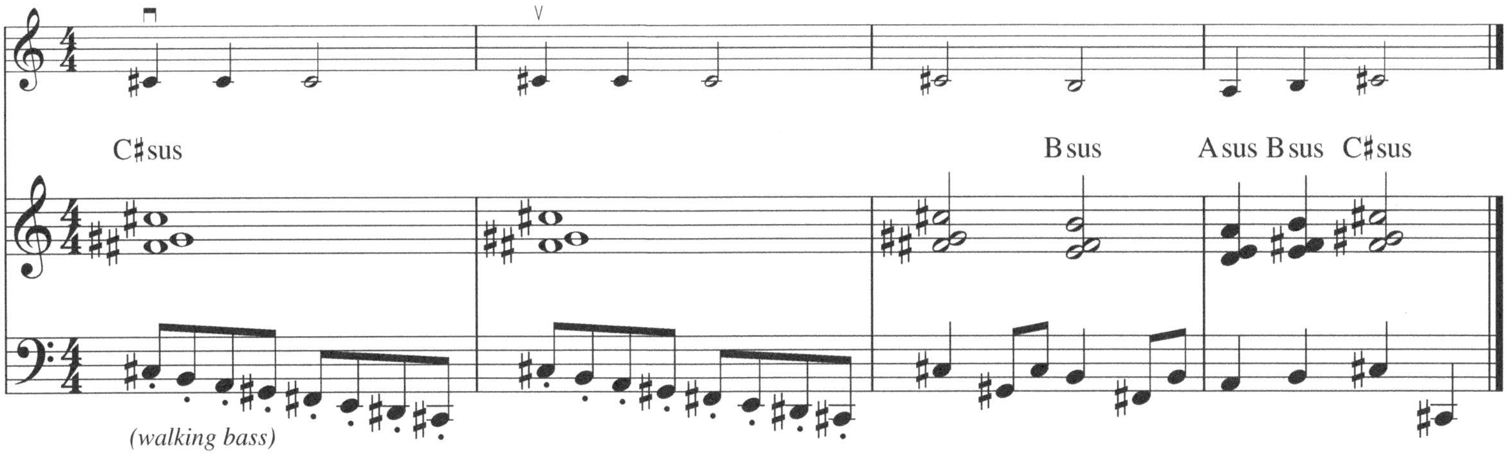

C♯sus Bsus Asus Bsus C♯sus

(walking bass)

49. STAY SHARP

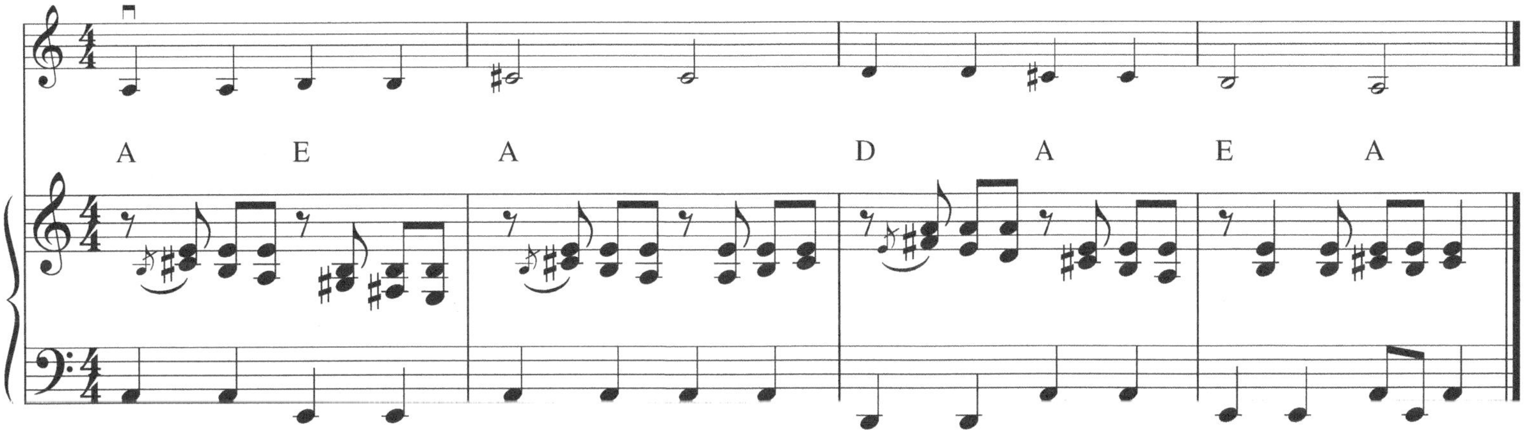

A E A D A E A

50. AT PIERROT'S DOOR

French Folk Song

Student books have repeats, not 1st and 2nd endings.

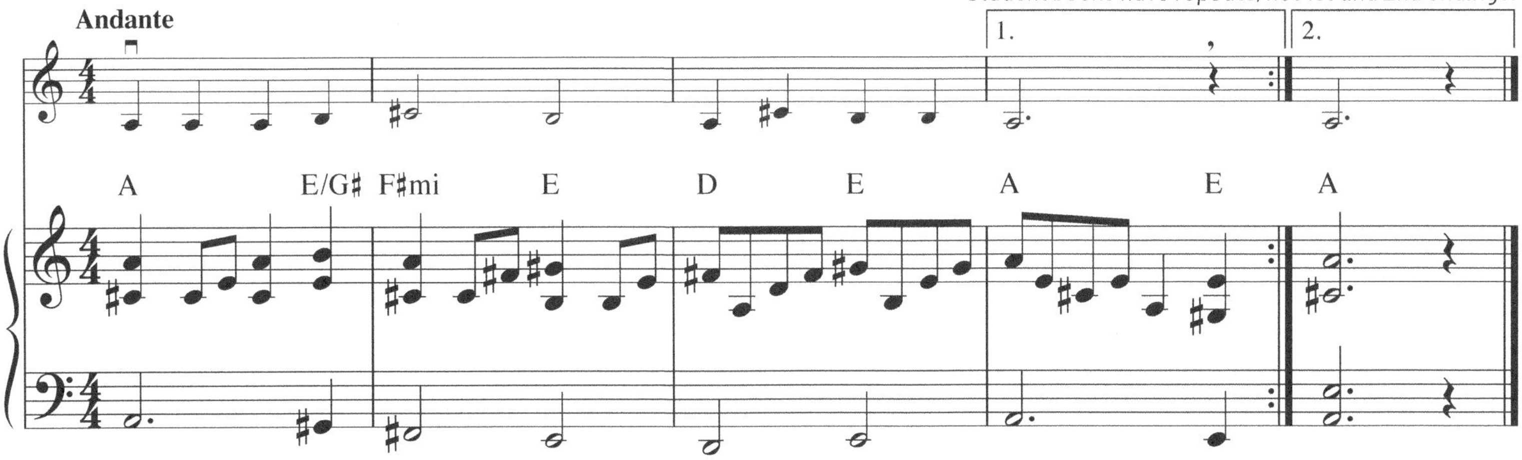

Andante

1. 2.

A E/G♯ F♯mi E D E A E A

52. LET'S READ "G♯" (G-sharp)

53. REACHING OUT

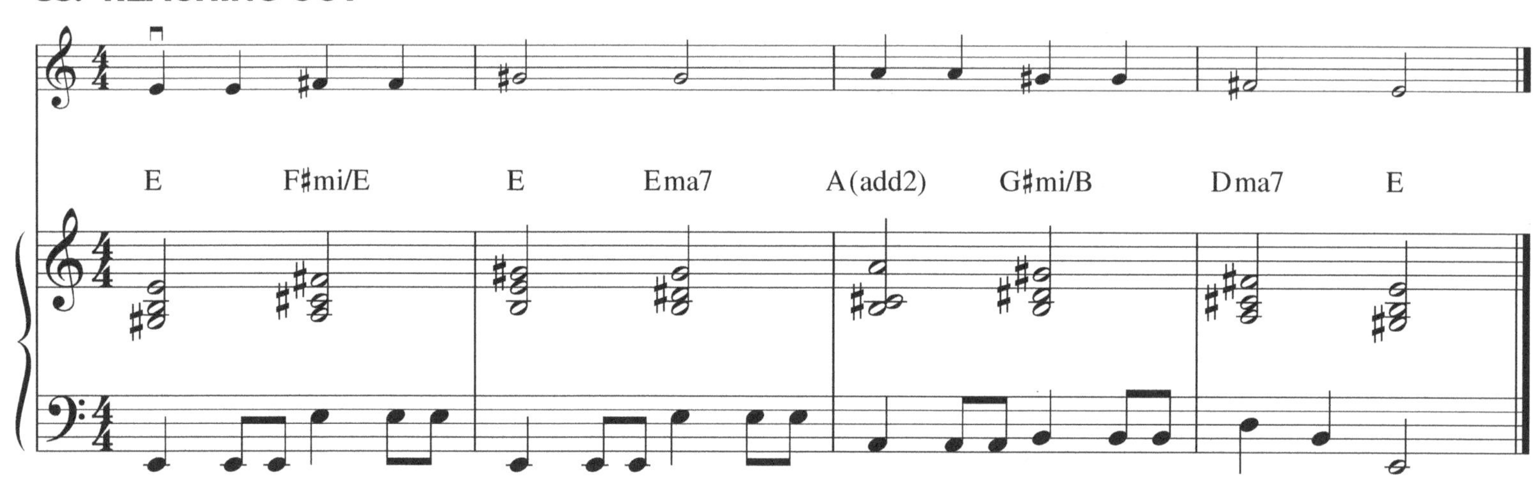

54. HIGHER AND HIGHER

55. A MAJOR SCALE

56. ESSENTIAL ELEMENTS QUIZ – A SONG FOR ANNE

Moderato

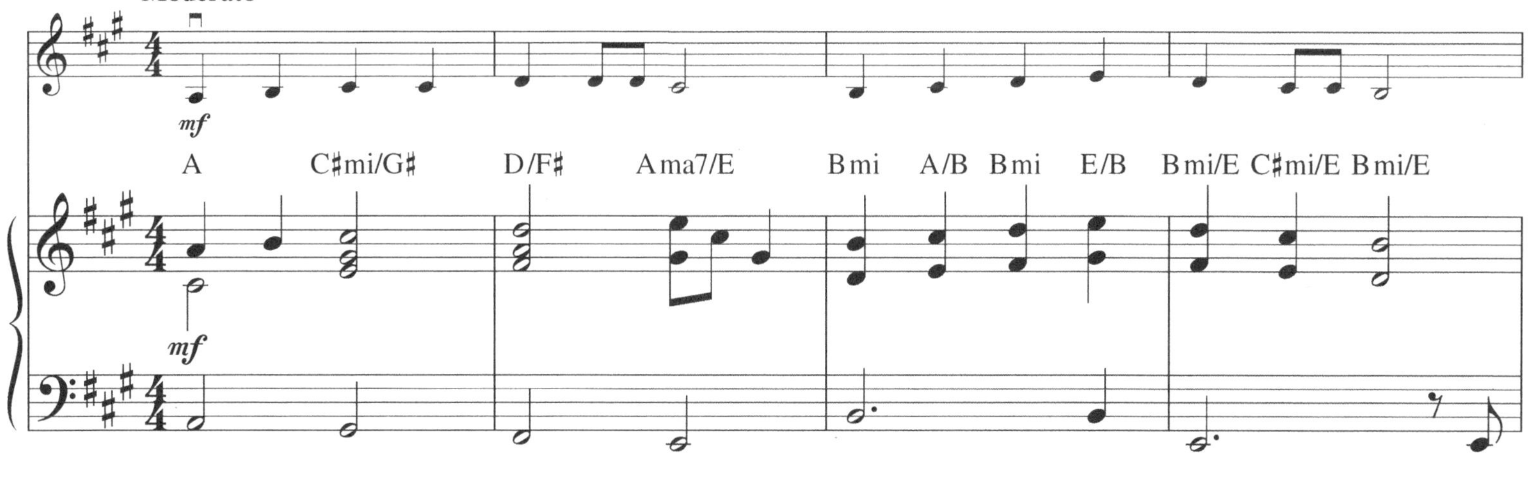

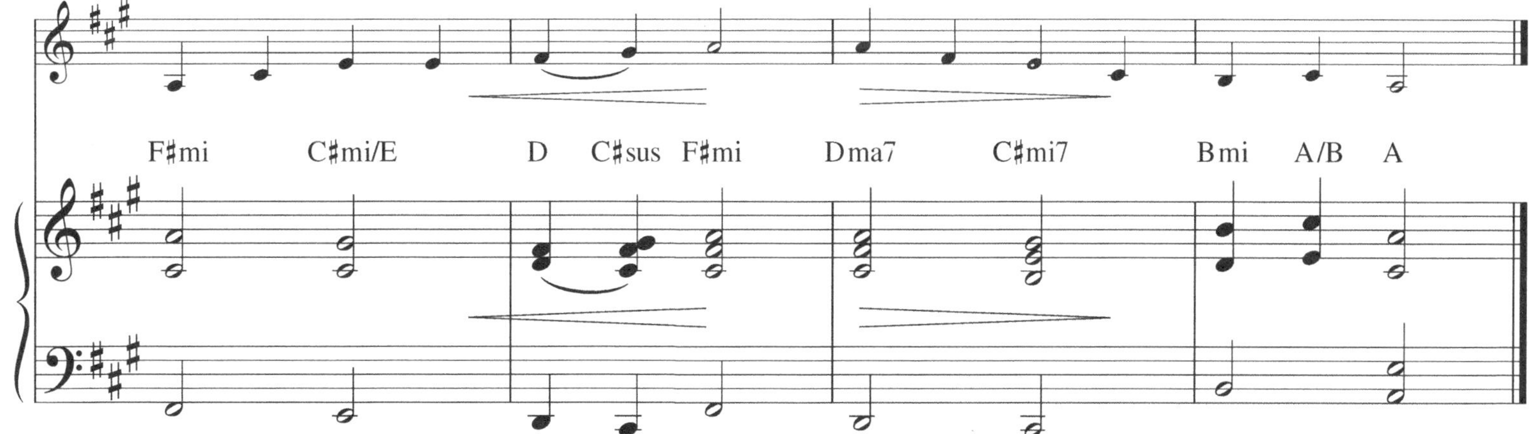

SHARP KEYS

57. LET'S READ "F♯" (F-sharp) – Review

58. HIGH POINT

59. MAGNIFICENT MONTANA

60. D MAJOR SCALE – Round

61. RUSSIAN FOLK TUNE

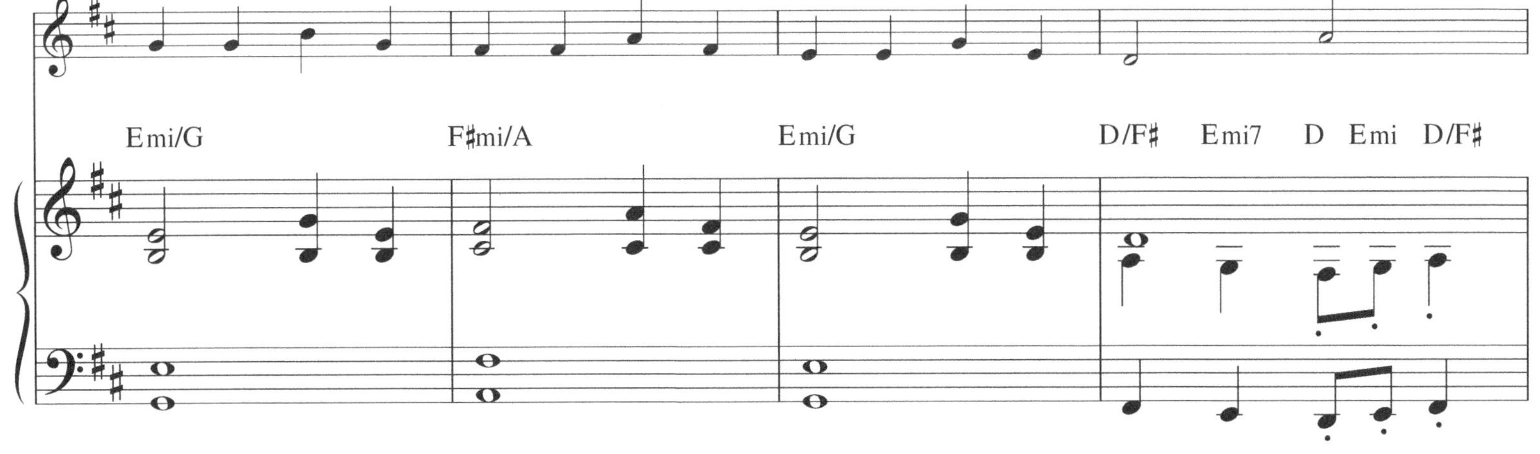

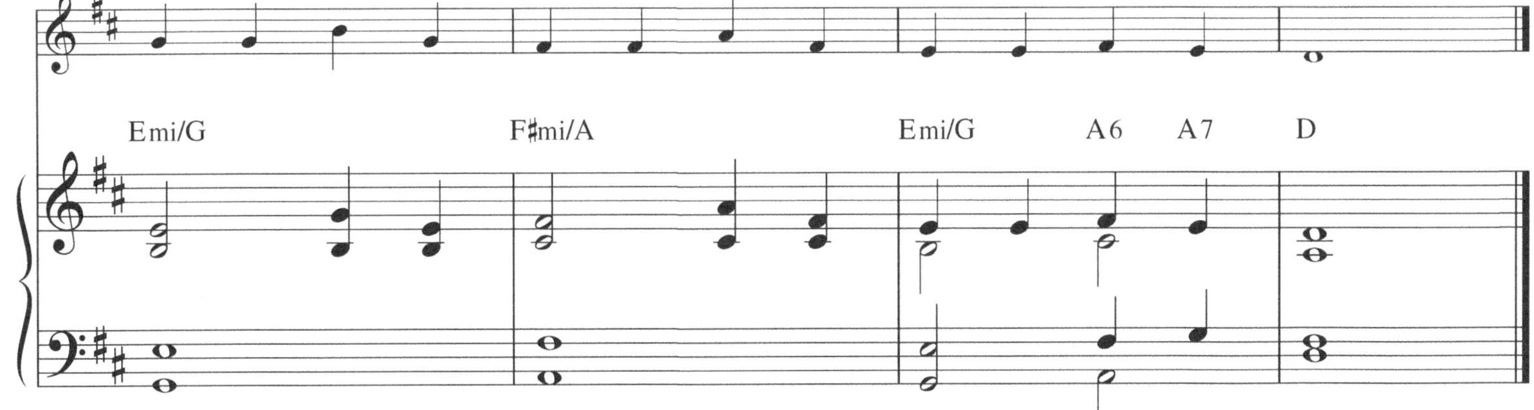

62. LET'S READ "G♯" (G-sharp)
G♯sus G♯ Esus Ema7 D(add2) E(add2) D(add2)/A E/A A
63. A MAJOR SCALE
A5 A2 A G/A E D/E E A
D E/D Bmi A/C♯ G/D A/E E A
64. A MAJOR ARPEGGIO
A A/G♯ F♯mi7 A/E Dma9 A(add2) A Dma7 Dma7/E A(add2)

SHARP KEYS
65. THE FIG TREE
Allegretto
f
decresc.
p
A
E/A
D/A
C♯mi/E
D/F♯
A ma7/E
B mi7/E
A
f
decresc.
p
cresc.
f
D(add2)
C♯7sus
C♯7
F♯mi7
B mi7
A/E
D/E
E7
A(add2)
cresc.
f
66. SITKA CITY
Moderato
Russian Folk Song
mf
p
A
D
A sus A
D
A sus A
mf
p
f
A5
E/D D
E7
A sus A
A5
E/D
D
E7
E7/A A
f

RHYTHMS

67. RHYTHM RAP
Student books have repeats, not 1st and 2nd endings.
1.
2.
D5
C/D
D
C/D
D
C/D
D5
D5
68. SIXTEENTH NOTE FANFARE
Student books have repeats, not 1st and 2nd endings.
1.
2.
D5
C/D
D
C/D
D
C/D
D5
D5
69. TECHNIQUE TRAX
G
A
G
D
G
D
A
D
70. SWEET SIXTEENTHS
Allegretto
D
A7

D
71. MOCKINGBIRD
Moderato
Alice Hawthorne (Septimus Winner) (1827–1902)
mf
Dma7/A
Gma7/A Emi7/A
Dma7/A
Emi7/A
mf
p
Dma7
A7(♯11)
Gma7
F♯7(♭5)
f
Bmi7
E9
G/A
Gma7/A
E♭ma9
D
RHYTHMS

72. RHYTHM RAP

Student books have repeats, not 1st and 2nd endings.

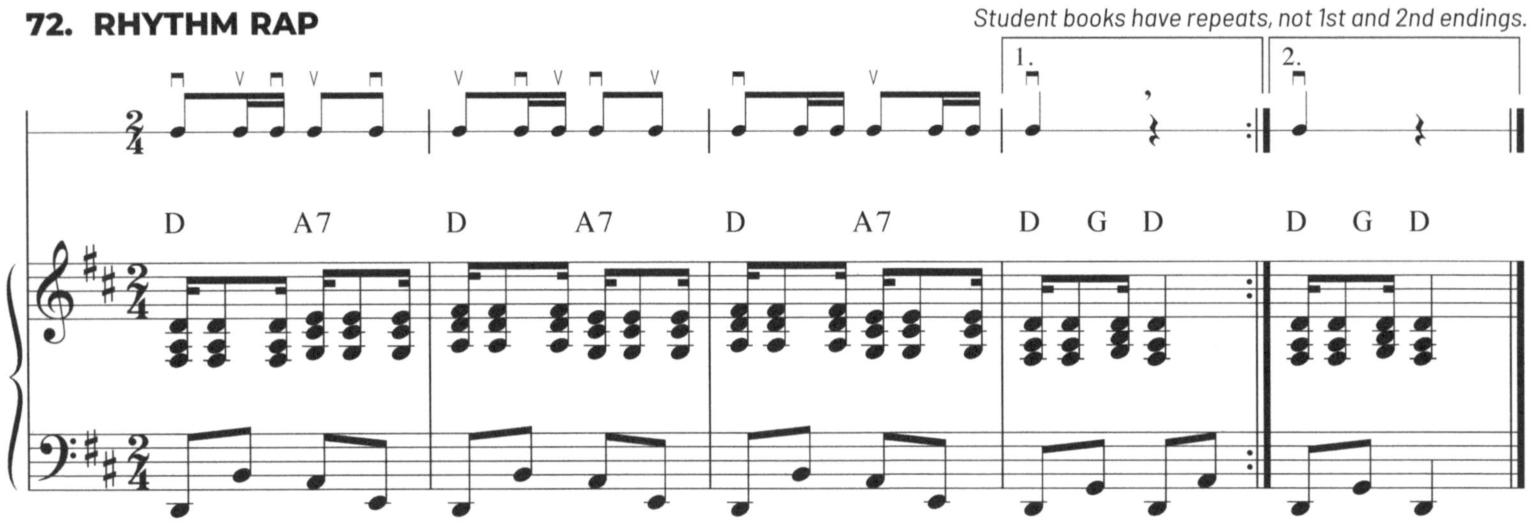

RHYTHMS

73. BLUEBERRY PIE

Student books have repeats, not 1st and 2nd endings.

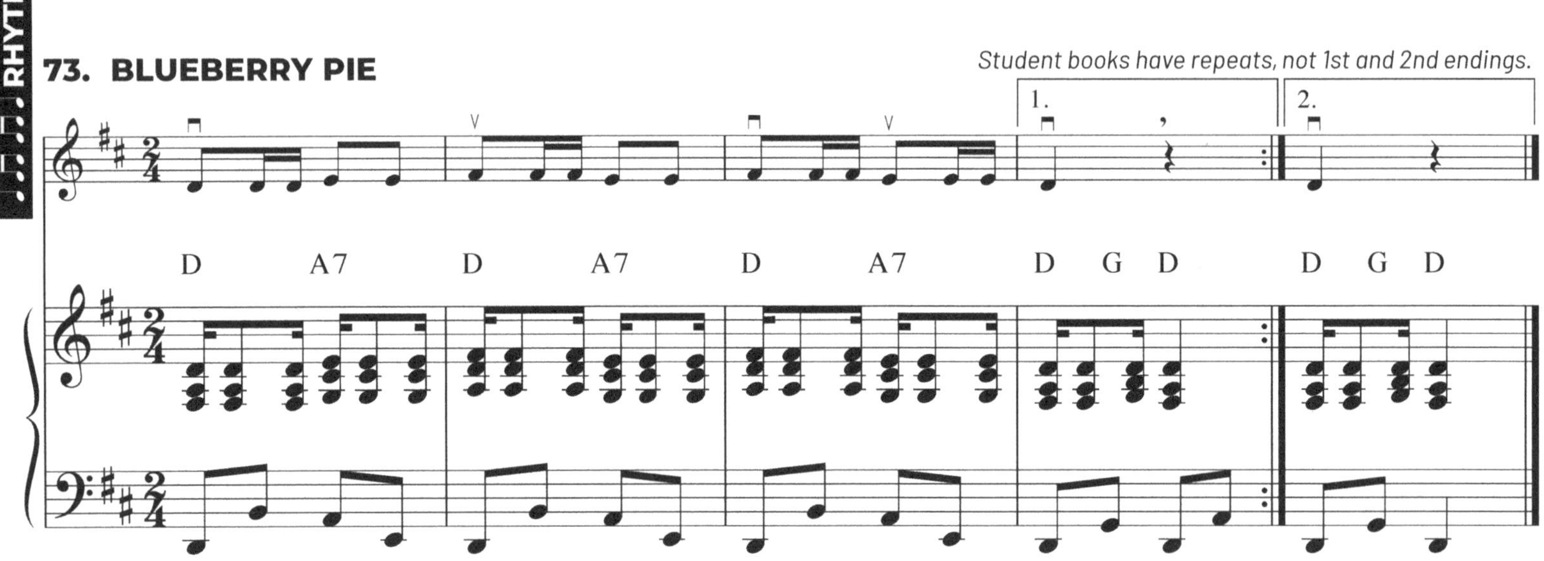

74. TECHNIQUE TRAX

75. RHYTHM RAP

Student books have repeats, not 1st and 2nd endings.

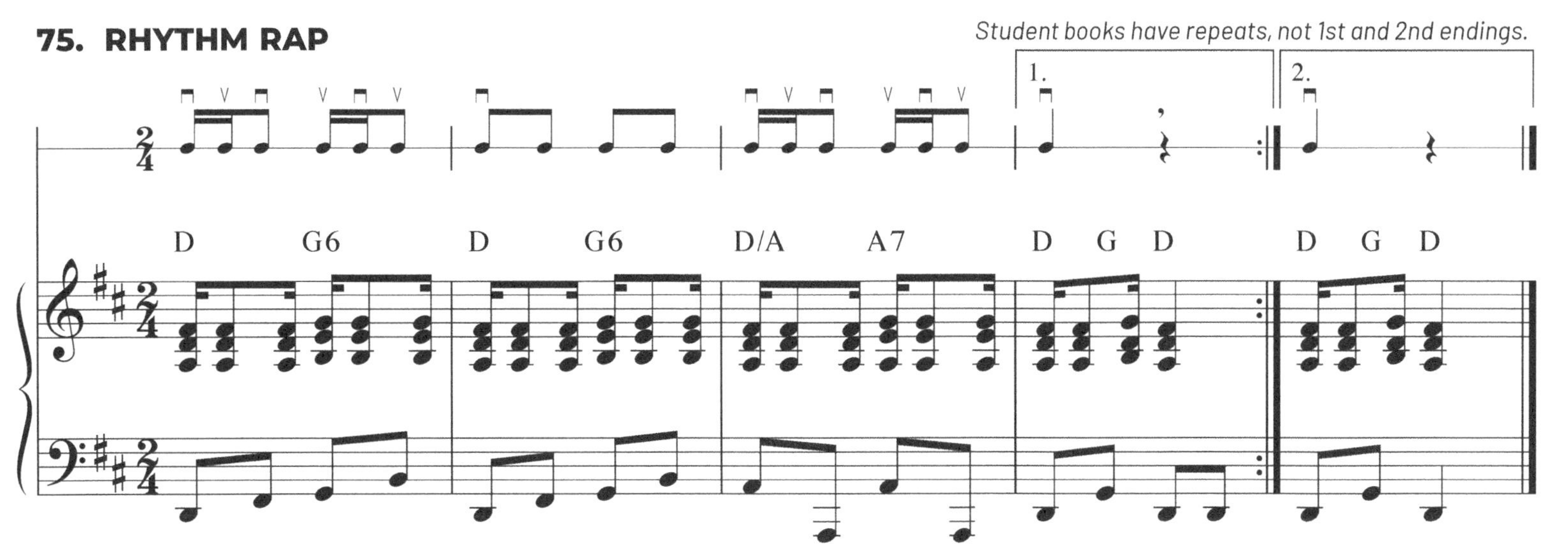

76. MARCHING ALONG

Student books have repeats, not 1st and 2nd endings.

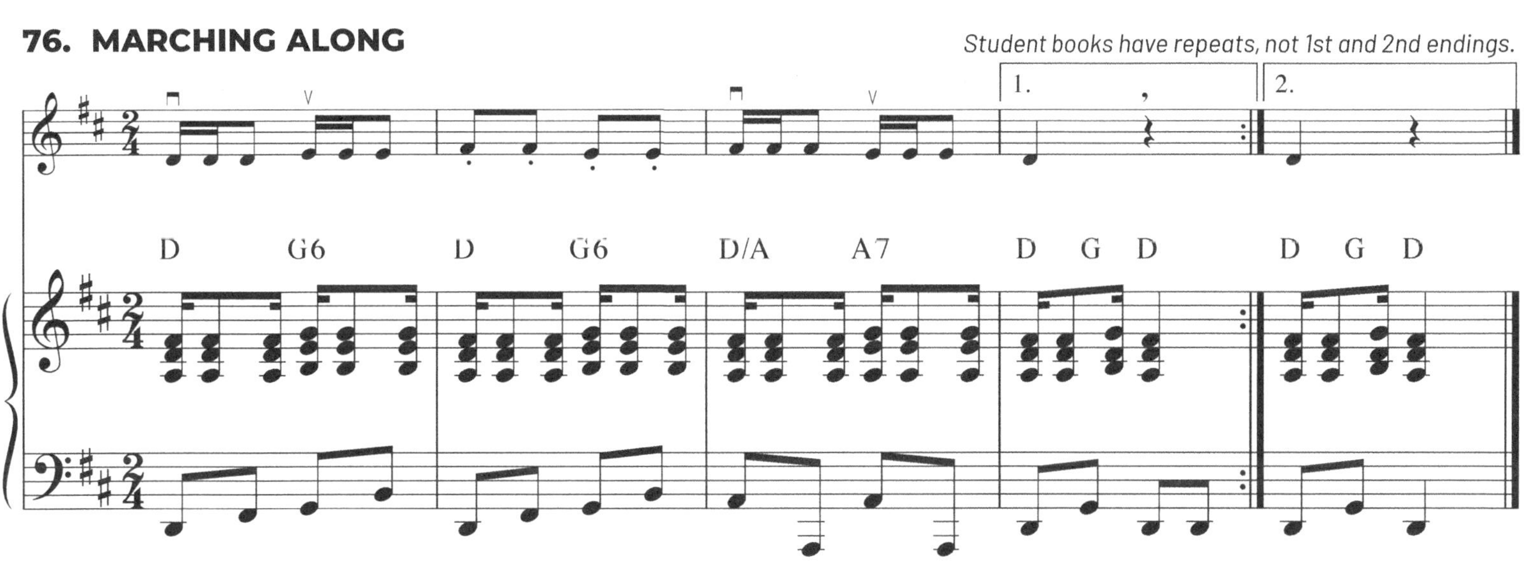

77. ON THE MOVE

RHYTHMS

78. RHYTHM ETUDE – Duet

79. ESSENTIAL ELEMENTS QUIZ – RHYTHM ROUND-UP

80. RHYTHM RAP
Student books have repeats, not 1st and 2nd endings.
1.
2.
D Ami7 D Ami7 D Ami7 D
81. TECHNIQUE TRAX
Student books have repeats, not 1st and 2nd endings.
1.
2.
D Ami7 D Ami7 D Ami7 D
RHYTHMS
82. HOOKED ON D MAJOR
D Asus A D/F♯ C/G G D/A G/A E/A A A/G Gsus2 D
Gsus2 A/G G A/G C D Asus A D

83. THE MOUNTAIN CLIMBER

84. KEEP IT SHORT

85. ESSENTIAL CREATIVITY – writing assignment in student books.

86. RHYTHM RAP
Student books have repeats, not 1st and 2nd endings.
1.
2.
D G6 D Bmi G/E D/E A7 D G/A D
87. SYNCOPATION TIME
Student books have repeats, not 1st and 2nd endings.
1.
2.
D G6 D Bmi G/E D/E A7 D G/A D
RHYTHMS
88. MIRROR IMAGE
Gsus2 A/G Emi7 F♯mi7 Emi7 F♯mi/A Emi/A D
89. CHILDREN'S SHOES
African American Spiritual
D7 F♯7 G7 D7 Bmi7 E9 E6 E7 A7 G7 D7

RHYTHMS

90. HOOKED ON SYNCOPATION

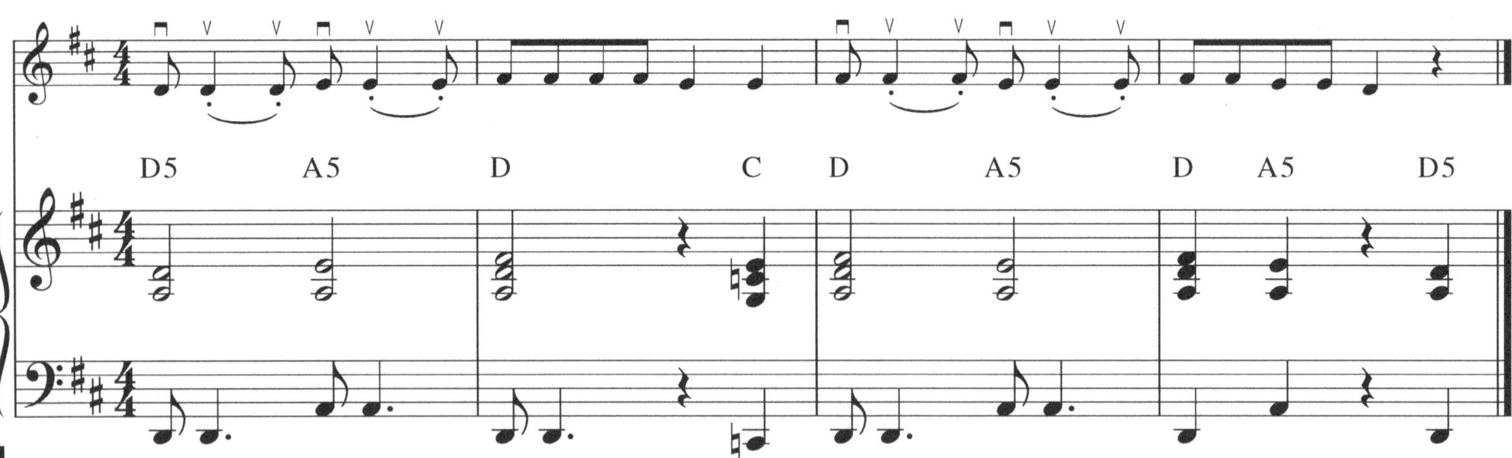

91. ESSENTIAL ELEMENTS QUIZ – TOM DOOLEY

FLAT KEYS

92. LET'S READ "B♭" (B-flat)

93. ROLLING ALONG

94. MATCHING OCTAVES

95. LET'S READ "F" (F-natural)

96. TECHNIQUE TRAX

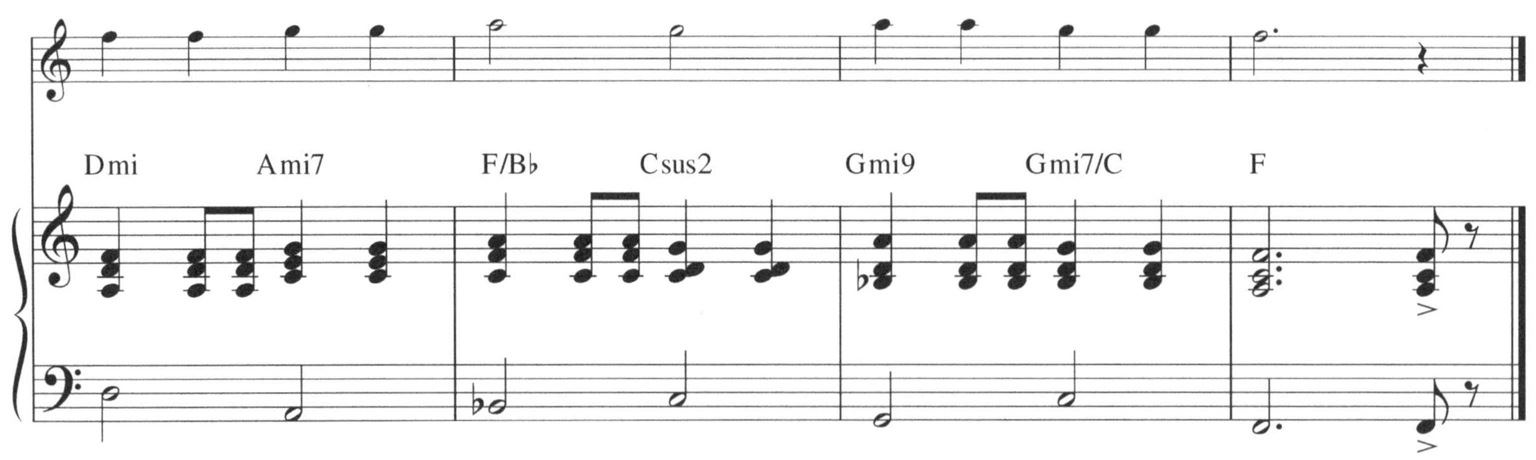

97. F MAJOR SCALE

98. THEME FROM VIOLIN CONCERTO

Ludwig van Beethoven (1770–1827)

FLAT KEYS
99. LET'S READ "E♭" (E-flat)
E♭ A7(♭5) A♭ma7 D♭9 Cmi7 F6 A♭ma7/B♭ Fmi7/B♭ E♭
100. HOT CROSS BUNS
E♭ B♭7 E♭ E♭ B♭7 E♭ A♭ B♭ E♭ B♭7 E♭
101. LET'S READ "B♭" (B-flat)
B♭7 E♭7 B♭7 F7 B♭7 F7 B♭7
102. VIKING WAY
Gmi Fsus2/G Gmi E♭ma9 Dmi9 Gmi F/G Gmi

FLAT KEYS

103. HIKING ALONG

104. B♭ MAJOR SCALE

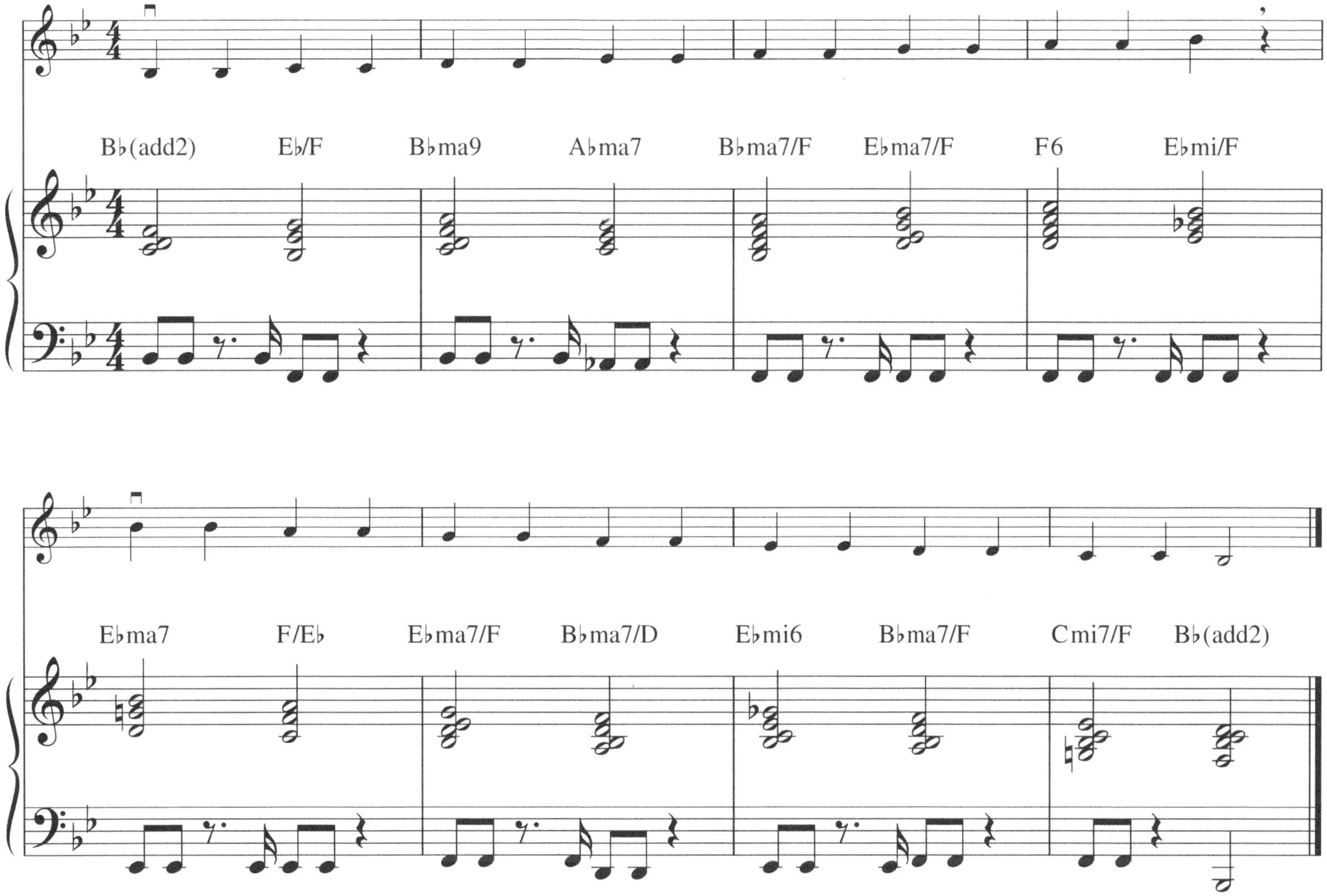

B♭(add2) E♭/F B♭ma9 A♭ma7 B♭ma7/F E♭ma7/F F6 E♭mi/F

E♭ma7 F/E♭ E♭ma7/F B♭ma7/D E♭mi6 B♭ma7/F Cmi7/F B♭(add2)

105. SLOVAKIAN FOLK SONG

Allegro

mf

B♭ F7 B♭ F7 B♭

mf

Gmi E♭ C7 F7 B♭ F7 B♭

106. CAVALIER COUNTRY

Gmi Dmi E♭ B♭ E♭ Cmi Fsus F

Gmi Dmi E♭ B♭ E♭ B♭ F B♭

107. ESSENTIAL ELEMENTS QUIZ – AYN KAYLOKAYNU
Andantino
Traditional Jewish Song
mp
mf
B♭
F7
B♭
F7
B♭
rit.
a tempo
E♭
Cmi
B♭/F
F7
B♭
108. LET'S READ "E♭" (E-flat)
E♭
E♭/G
Cmi
E♭/B♭
Fmi7
Gmi7
Fmi7
B♭/F
E♭
109. TECHNIQUE TRAX
Cmi7 Gmi/C Cmi7
B♭5 B♭sus2 Gmi
A♭ma7 Gsus/A♭ Fmi
A♭/B♭ B♭ E♭

FLAT KEYS

110. LET'S READ "B♭" (B-flat)
B♭
E♭6/B♭
B♭
B♭ma7/D
E♭
F/E♭
B♭
111. TECHNIQUE BUILDER
B♭
F
E♭
F
E♭
F
B♭
F
E♭
B♭
E♭
F
B♭
112. B♭ MAJOR SCALE
B♭
F sus
F
B♭/D
E♭
B♭
E♭
F
B♭sus
B♭
Gmi
F/G
E♭/G
F/G
E♭sus
E♭
B♭
F sus
B♭

113. THE MOUNTAIN DEER CHASE

FLAT KEYS

114. ESSENTIAL CREATIVITY – RAKES OF MALLOW

117. HOOKED ON 6/8

118. ROW, ROW, ROW YOUR BOAT – Round

American Folk Round

119. SLURRING IN 6/8 TIME

120. JOLLY GOOD FELLOW

Andante

D G D A D A

D C G/B E/G♯ D/A A7 D

6/8 RHYTHMS

121. RHYTHM RAP

D5 A D Csus2 D Bmi G D

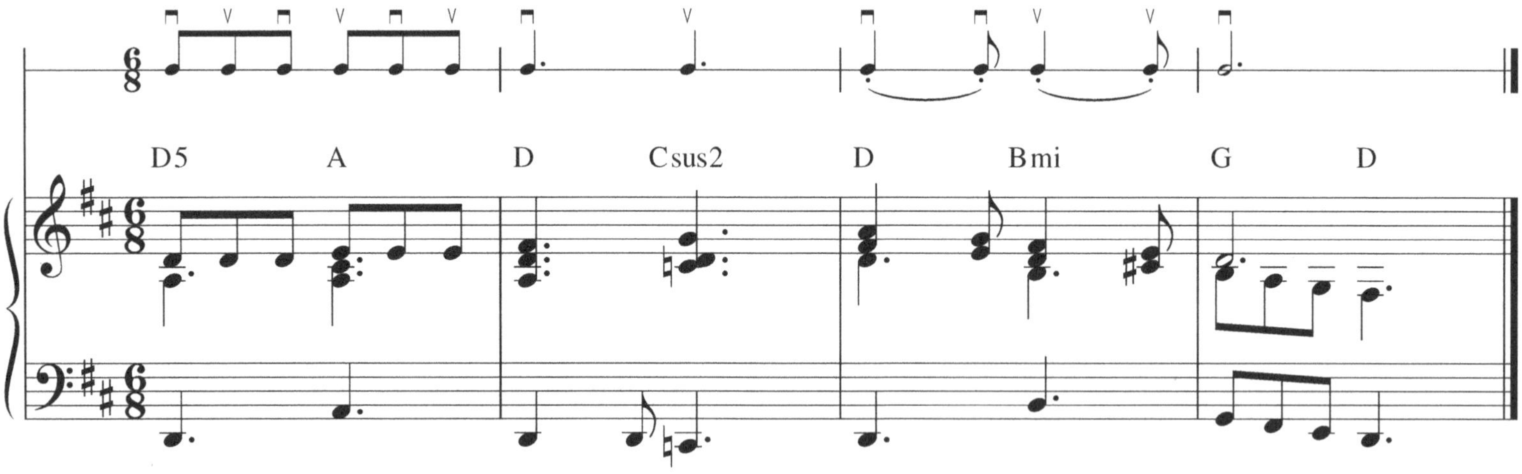

122. RISE AND FALL

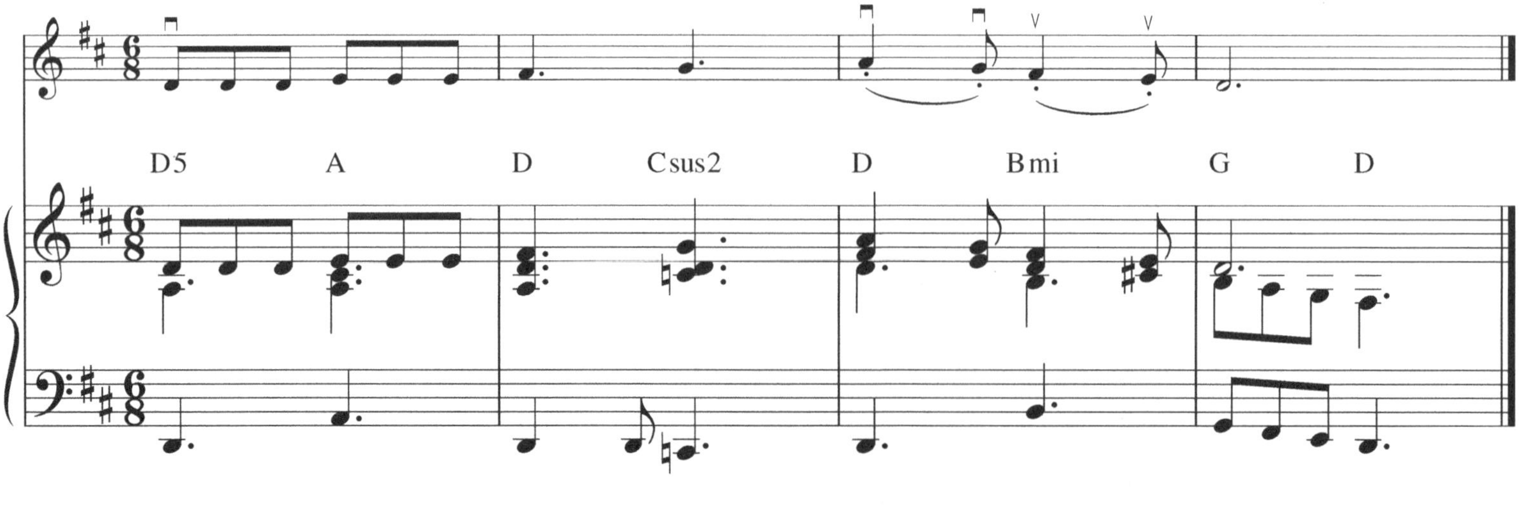

D5 A D Csus2 D Bmi G D

123. BEACH WALK
▲ Student books: Write in the correct time signature before you begin.
D
Bmi7
Esus
F♯mi/A
Emi
Ami/C
A
D
124. MAY TIME
Allegretto
W. A. Mozart (1756–1791)
mf
D
A/C♯
D
G/B
A/C♯
D
mf
A/C♯
D
Emi/G
A
D
G/B
A/C♯
D
Bmi
E/G♯
f
mf
p
A
D
D/F♯
G/B
Emi
D/A
A7
D
f
mf
p
6/8 RHYTHMS

125. D MINOR (Natural) SCALE

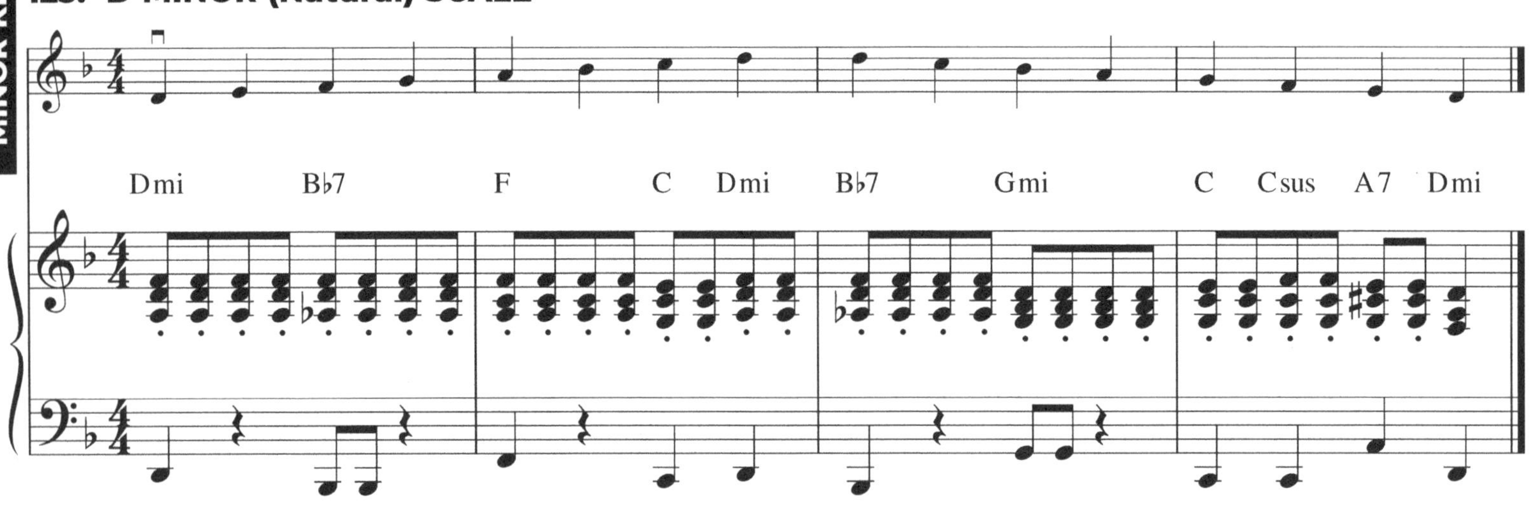

126. MAHLER'S THEME – Round

Andante

Gustav Mahler (1860–1911)

① *p* ② *mp*

Fmi

p *mp*

③ *mf* ④ *p*

F5

(Repeat as needed for round)

mf *p*

127. SHALOM CHAVERIM – Round
Andante
Hebrew Folk Song
mp
mf
mp
Fmi
A
Fmi
E
mp
mf
mp
1.
2.
(Group 2)
p
mp
Dma7
Fmi/C
C7sus
Dma7
E
Fmi
C7sus
Fmi
Fmi
p
mp
128. THE SNAKE CHARMER
Allegretto
D5
A5
D5

129. G MINOR (Natural) SCALE

130. HATIKVAH

Israeli National Anthem

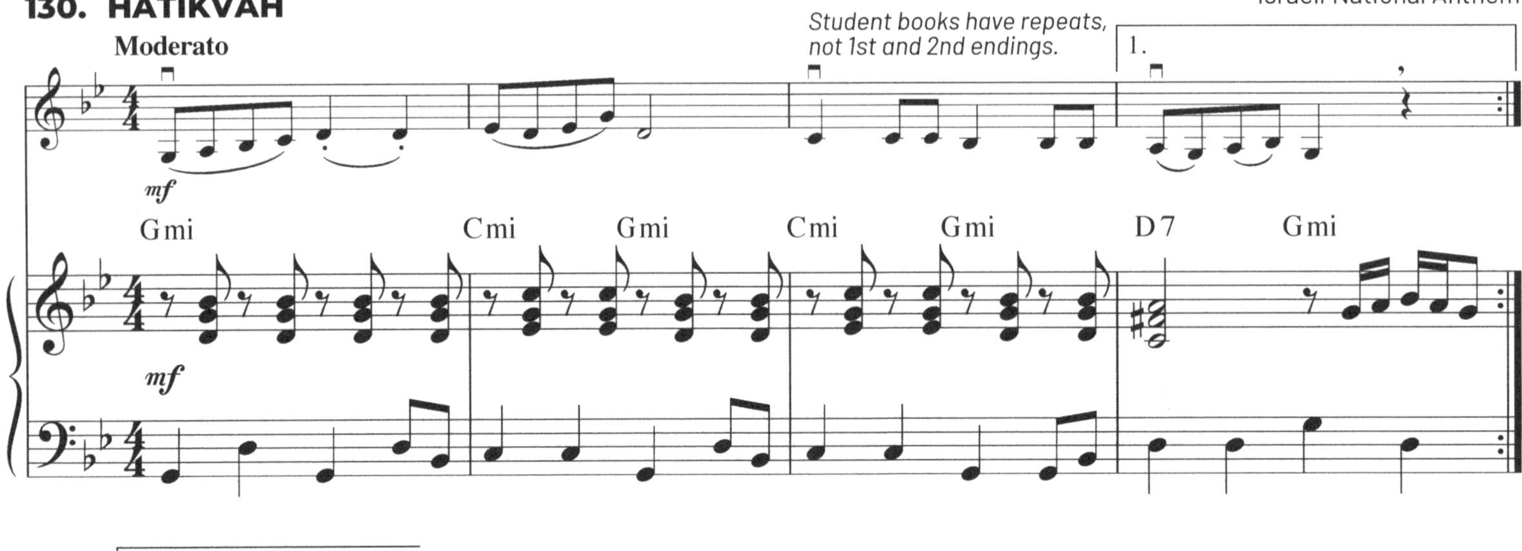

131. G MINOR (Natural) SCALE *(Upper Octave)*

132. ESSENTIAL ELEMENTS QUIZ – THE HANUKKAH SONG

Allegro

Israeli Folk Song

133. RHYTHM RAP

MIXED METER

134. FRENCH FOLK SONG

135. KUM BA YAH

African Spiritual

136. RHYTHM RAP

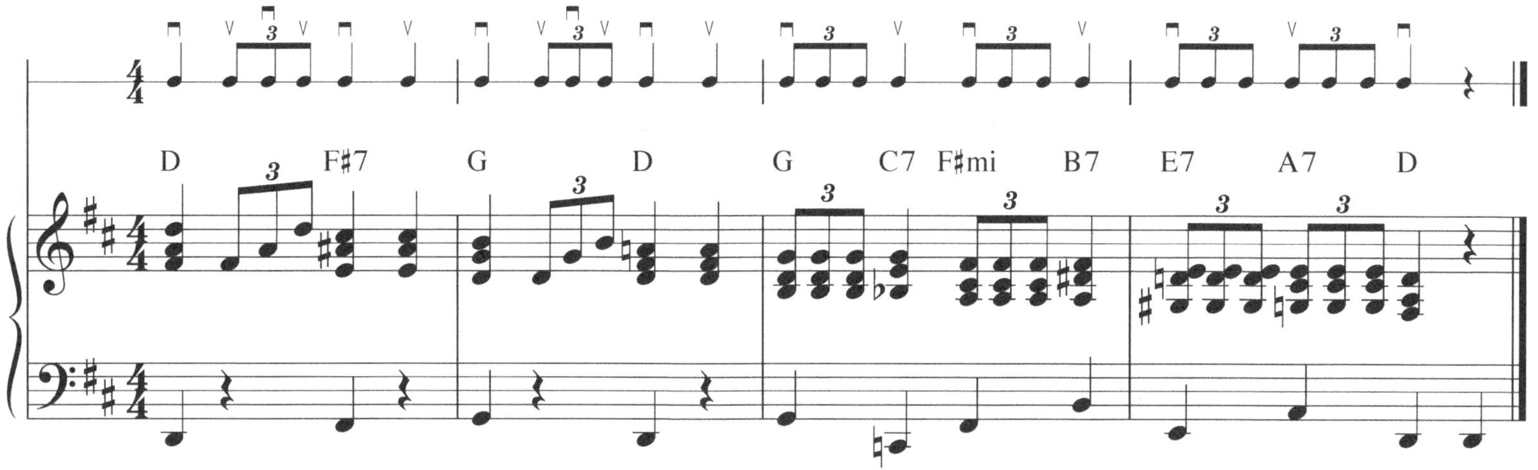

137. D MAJOR SCALE WITH TRIPLETS

138. ON THE MOVE

139. SLURRING TRIPLETS

RHYTHMS

140. TRIPLET ETUDE

141. LITTLE RIVER

142. FIELD SONG

Southern American Folk Song

144. A CUT ABOVE

D F♯7 G D B7

Emi D/A F♯mi/A A7sus A7 D G D

145. CUT TIME MARCH

G A7 D G A7 D Emi7 D/F♯

G D G D A7 D G D

146. RHYTHM RAP

147. SYNCOPATION MARCH

148. WHEN THE SAINTS GO MARCHIN' IN

James M. Black

149. RHYTHM RAP

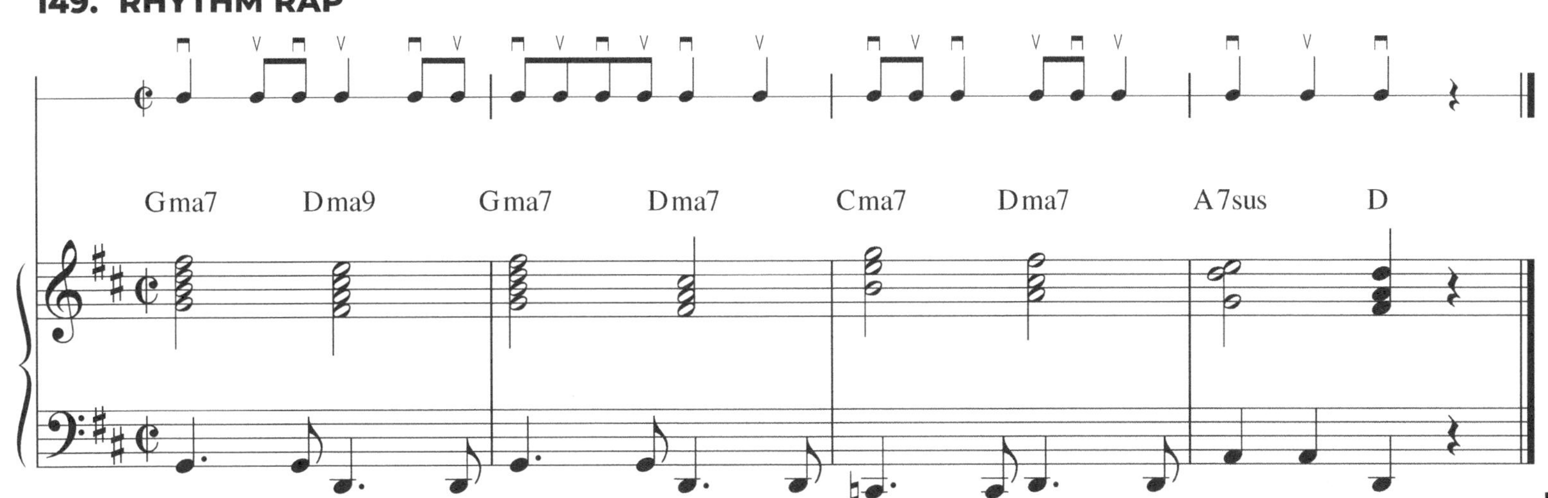

150. DOWN HOME

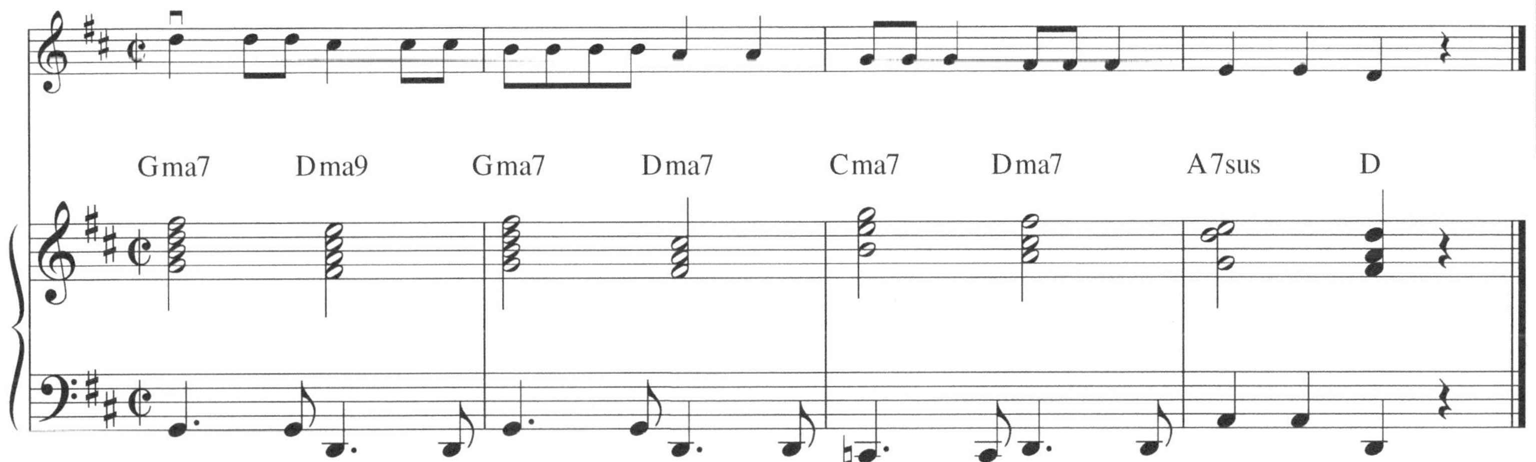

151. MOVING ALONG

152. RHYTHM RAP

153. UP TOWN

154. FLYING BOWS

155. MARCH FROM PEASANT'S CANTATA

J. S. Bach (1685–1750)

156. SAGEBRUSH OVERTURE – Orchestra Arrangement

Allegretto
23 "Yellow Rose of Texas"
A
B
mp
mp
G(add2) G G(add2) G G(add2) G G(add2) G/B
mp
f
f
G
f
Ami D7 Emi Ami/C G/D Cma7/D D C F(add2) G

157. POMP AND CIRCUMSTANCE – Orchestra Arrangement
Edward Elgar (1857–1933)
Arr. John Higgins
Moderato
A
B
mp - f
C G7 C F C Dmi7 G C D/C
1.
2.
G/B Emi Ami7 D7 G G7 F G7 C C7
PERFORMANCE SPOTLIGHT
11
rit.
F G/F C/E Ami Dmi7 F/G Emi/G Dmi/G C N.C.

158. AMERICA THE BEAUTIFUL – Orchestra Arrangement

Samuel Augustus Ward (1847–1903)
Arr. John Higgins

159. LA BAMBA – Duet

Mexican Folk Song
Arr. Michael Allen

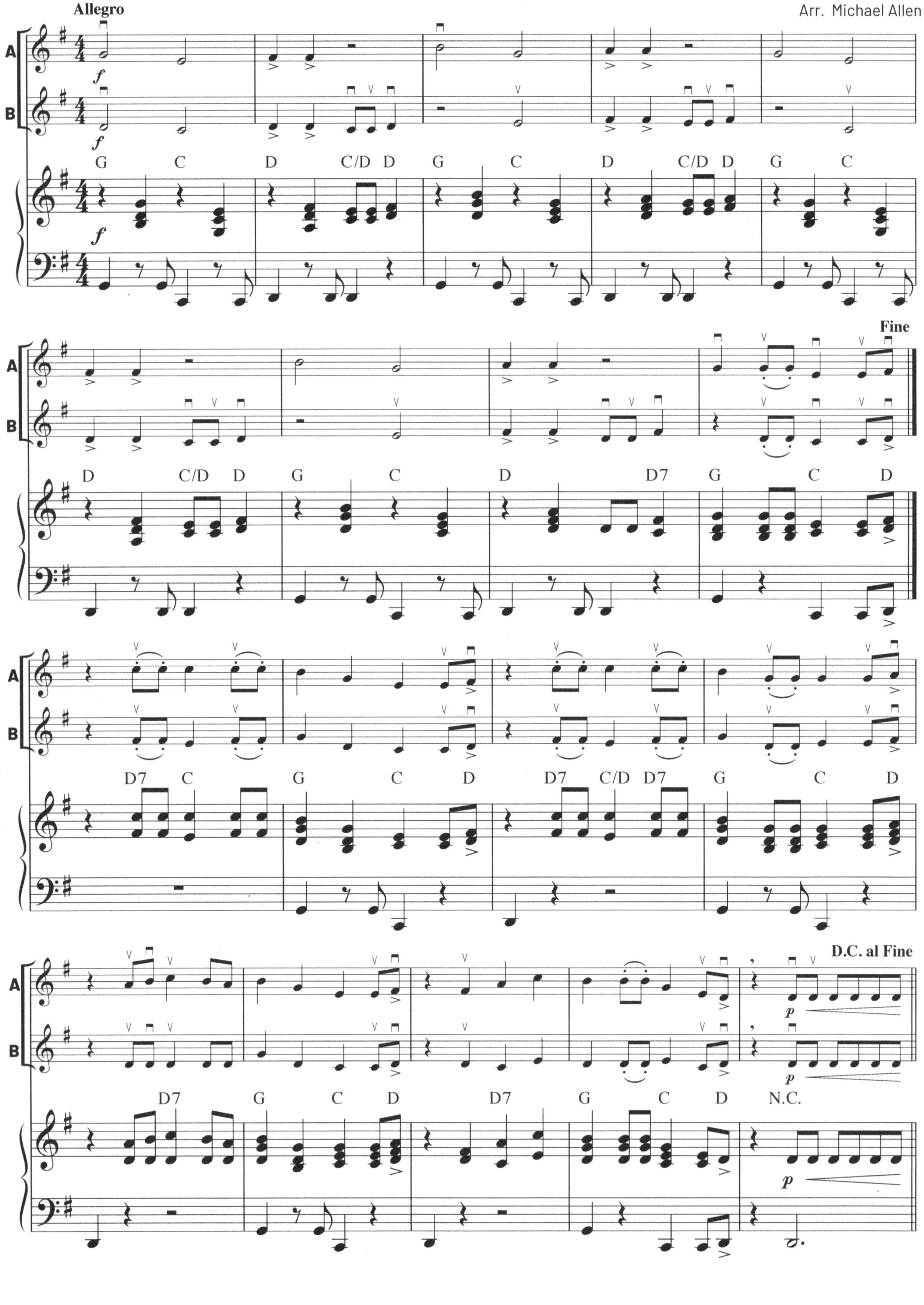

Allegro

A
B
G C D C/D D G C D C/D D G C

Fine

D C/D D G C D D7 G C D

D7 C G C D D7 C/D D7 G C D

D.C. al Fine

D7 G C D D7 G C D N.C.

160. IN THE BLEAK MIDWINTER – Orchestra Arrangement

Gustav Holst (1874–1934)
Arr. John Higgins

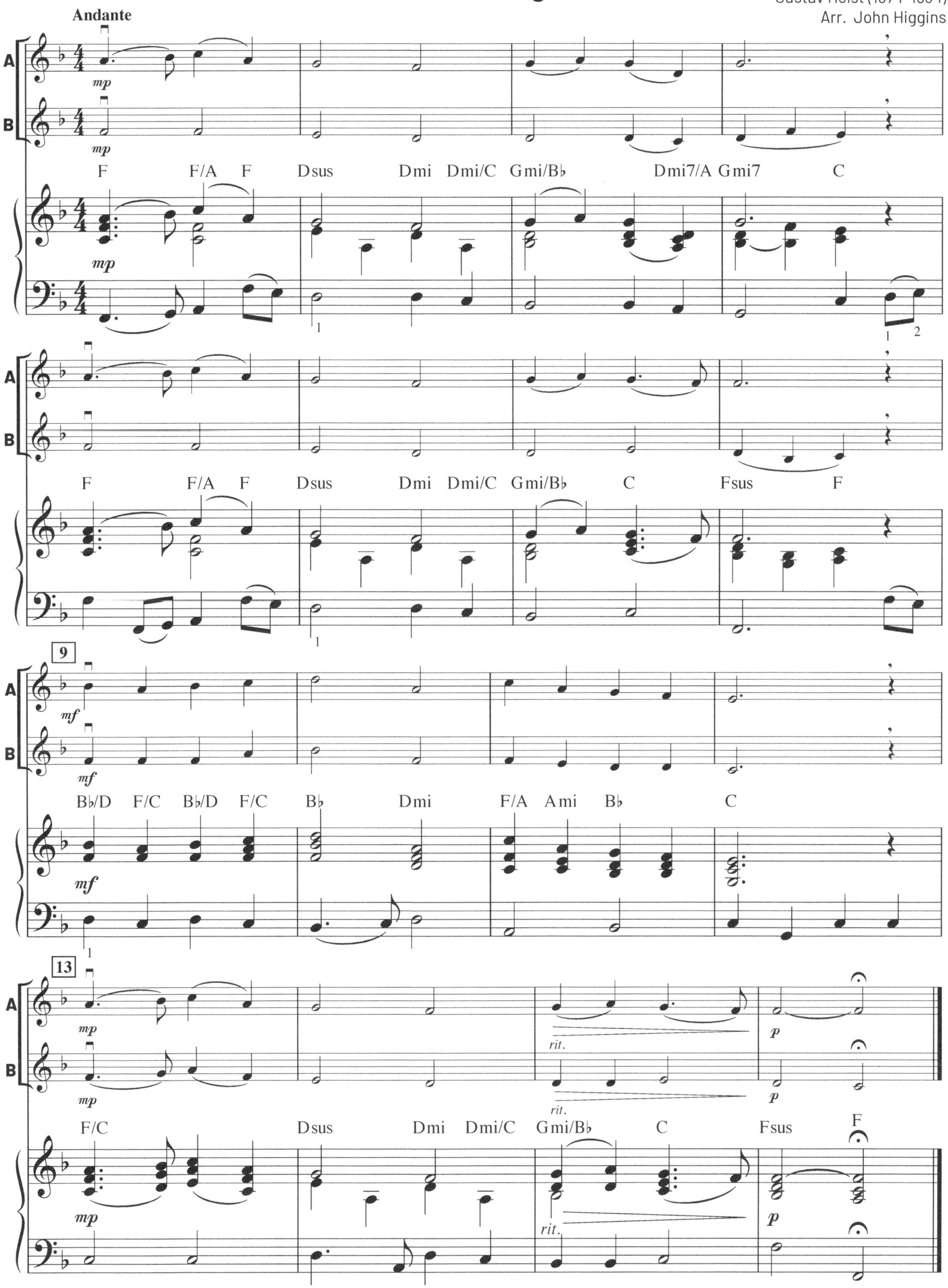
Andante
A
B
mp
F F/A F Dsus Dmi Dmi/C Gmi/B♭ Dmi7/A Gmi7 C
F F/A F Dsus Dmi Dmi/C Gmi/B♭ C Fsus F
9
mf
B♭/D F/C B♭/D F/C B♭ Dmi F/A Ami B♭ C
13
rit.
p
F/C Dsus Dmi Dmi/C Gmi/B♭ C Fsus F

PERFORMANCE SPOTLIGHT

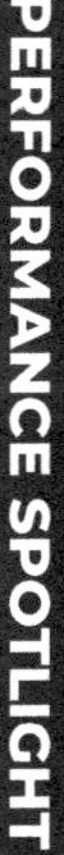

161. SWALLOWTAIL JIG – Orchestra Arrangement

Irish Jig
Arr. John Higgins

PERFORMANCE SPOTLIGHT

162. SIGHT-READING CHALLENGE #1

Andante

mp *cresc.*

Ami Emi/G F6 F/G Csus2 Emi F G7sus

mp *cresc.*

f

Ami Ami/G G/F Emi7 A7 Dmi7 A♭7 C/G G7sus Csus2

f

163. SIGHT-READING CHALLENGE #2

Lento

mf

A Bmi/A E D/F♯ E/G♯ A

mf

p

Bmi/D D/F♯ E Bmi7 E/G♯ D/F♯ E A

p

164. SIGHT-READING CHALLENGE #3

Allegretto

mf

B♭ F B♭ E♭ B♭ F B♭

mf

Gmi Dmi E♭ B♭ Gmi Dmi E♭ F B♭

165. SIGHT-READING CHALLENGE #4

Allegro

mp

F C F B♭ F B♭ C F

mp

mf

1. 2.

B♭ C B♭ F B♭ G7 C7 C7 F

mf

SIGHT-READING

166.
167.
168.
169.

HARMONICS/SHIFTING

174. 3–4 PATTERN

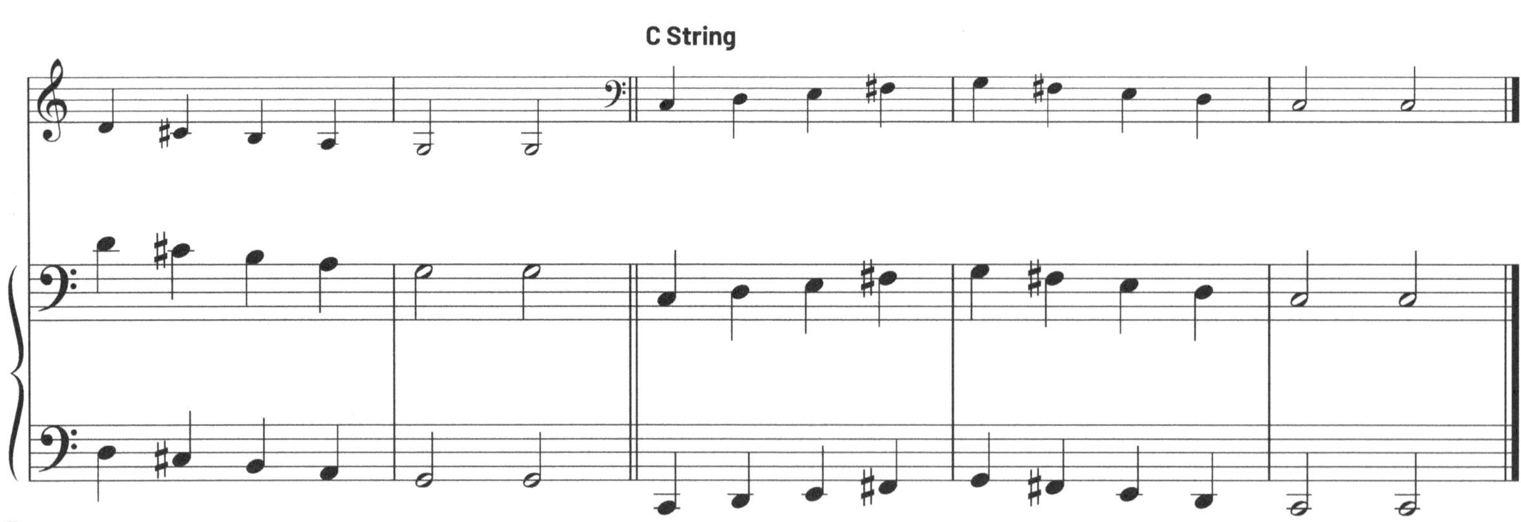

175. 2–3 PATTERN

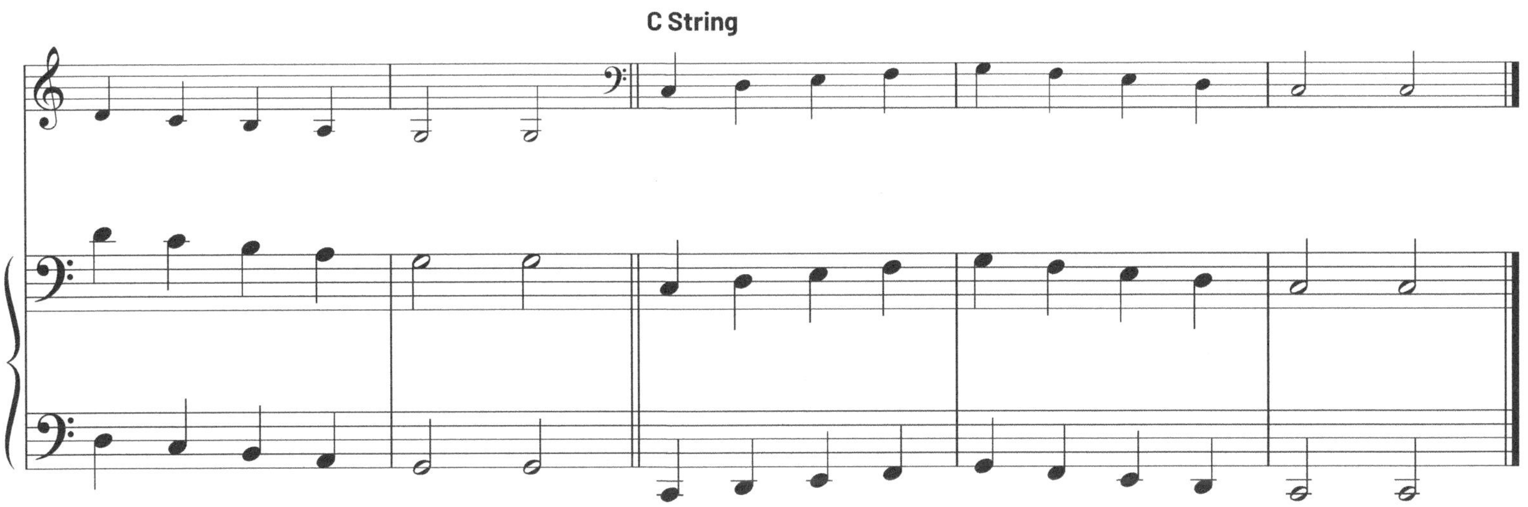

176. 1–2 PATTERN

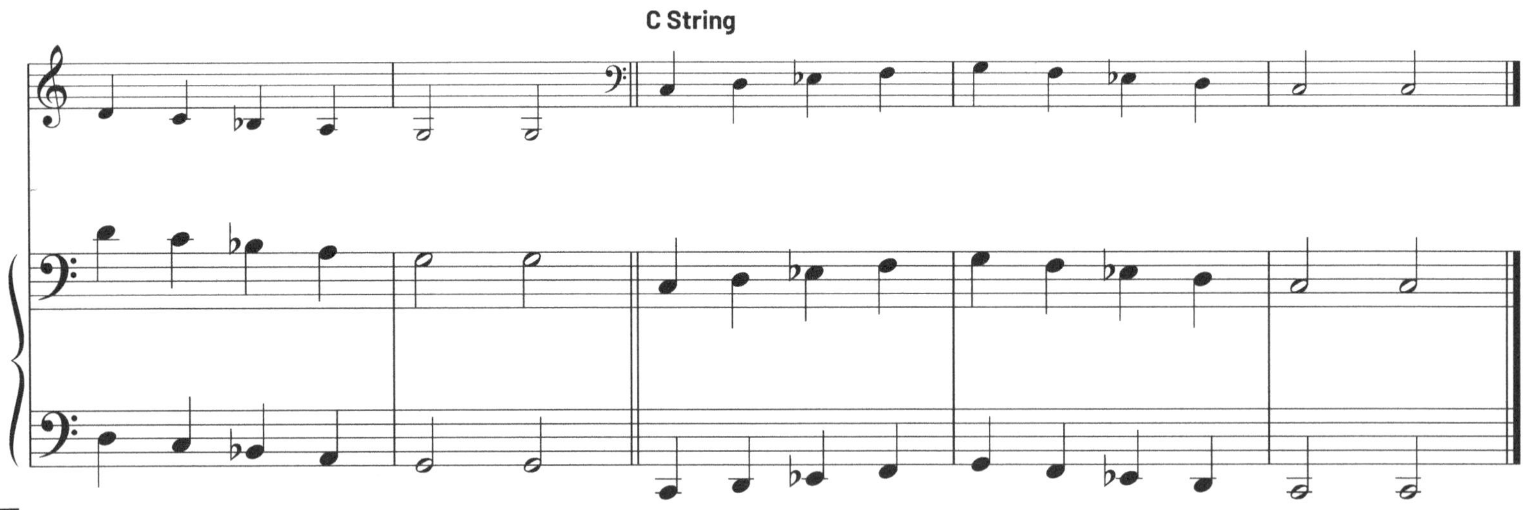

177. OPEN PATTERN

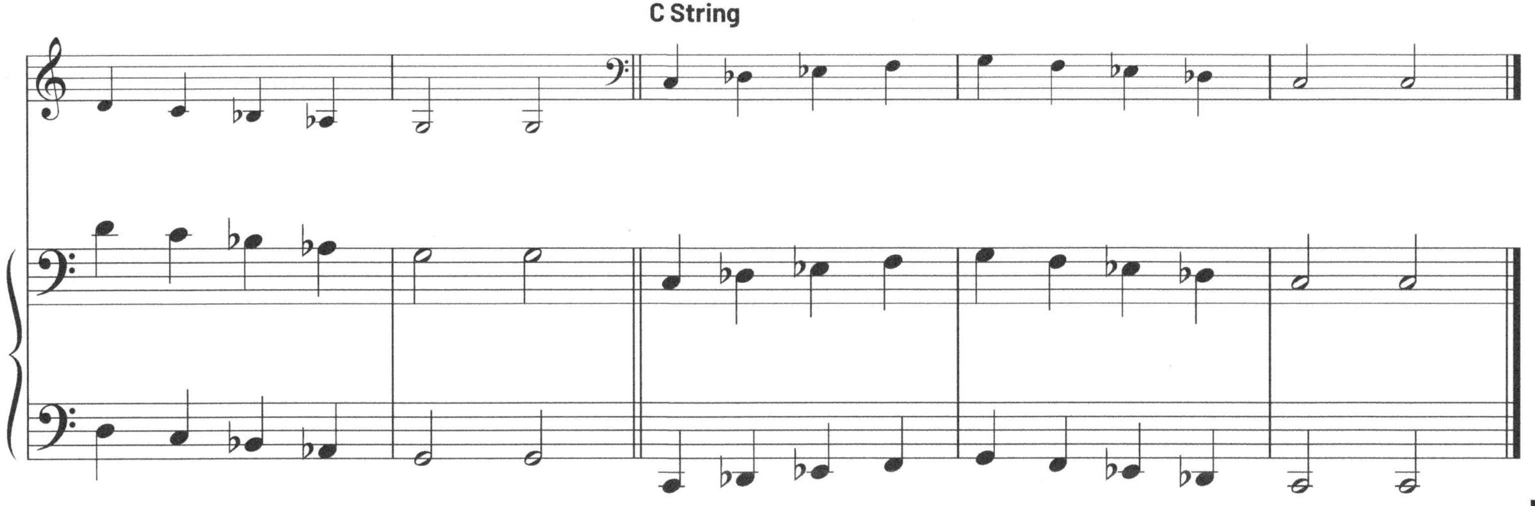

178. E STRING

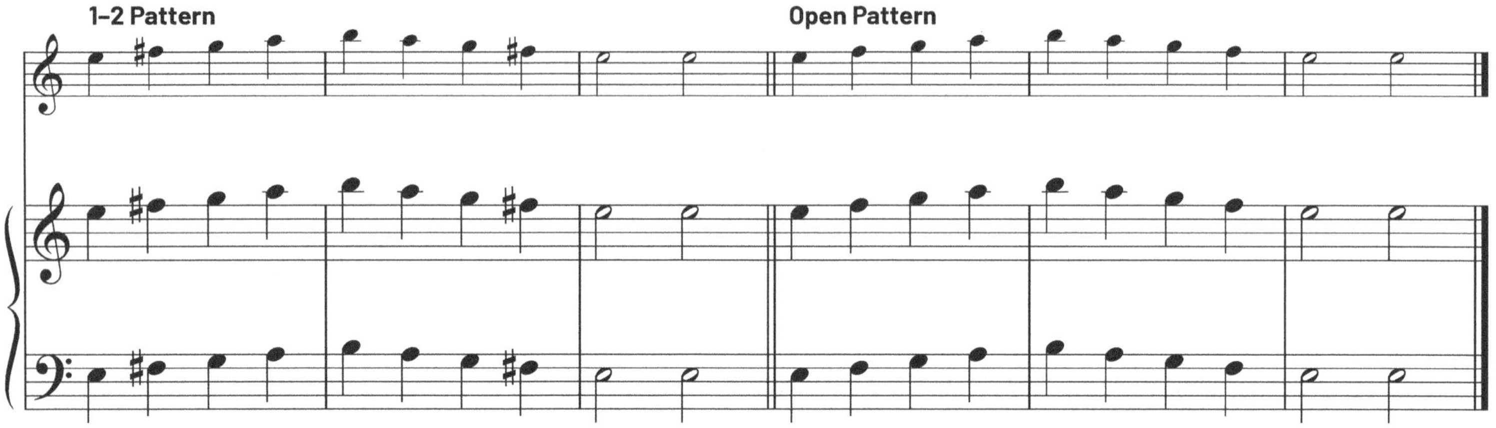

3–4 Pattern

2–3 Pattern

1–2 Pattern

Open Pattern

179. A STRING

3–4 Pattern

2–3 Pattern

1–2 Pattern

Open Pattern

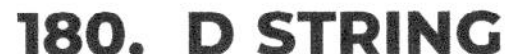

180. D STRING

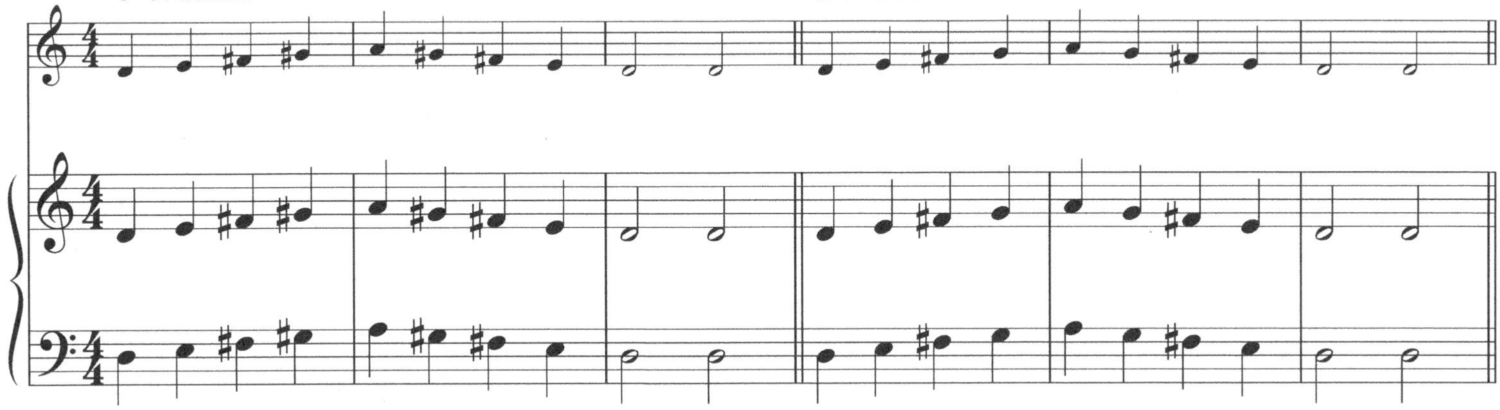
3–4 Pattern
2–3 Pattern

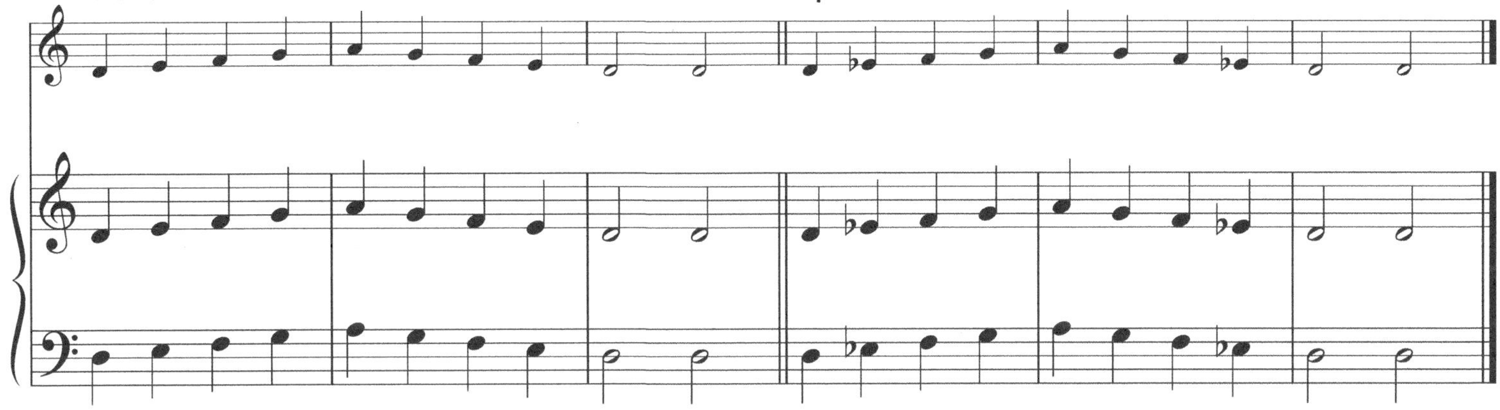
1–2 Pattern
Open Pattern

181. G STRING

3–4 Pattern
2–3 Pattern

1–2 Pattern
Open Pattern

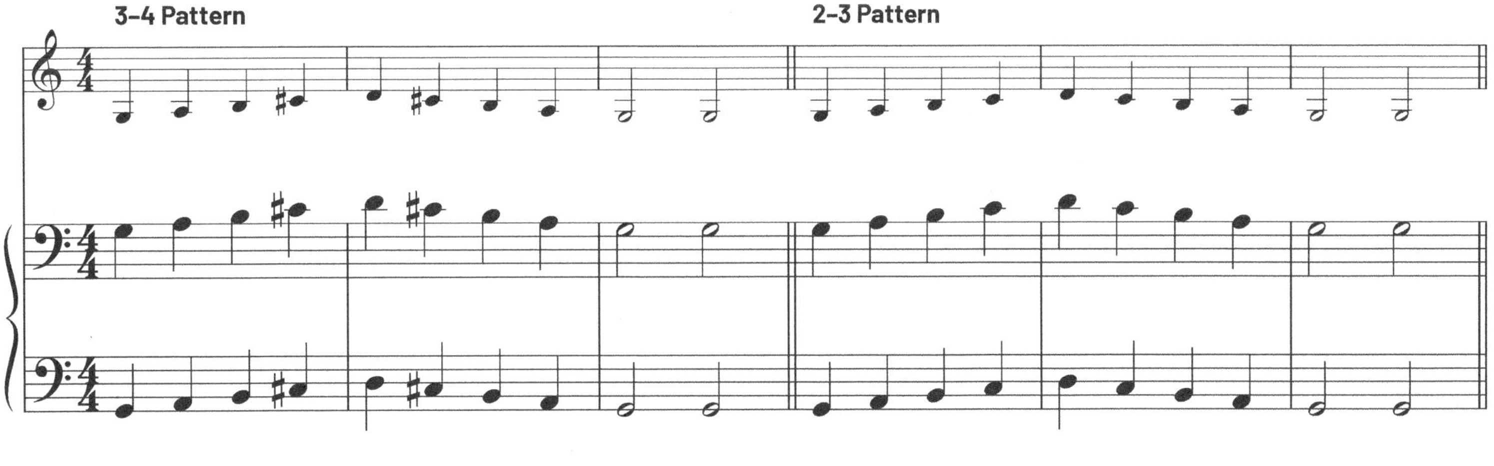

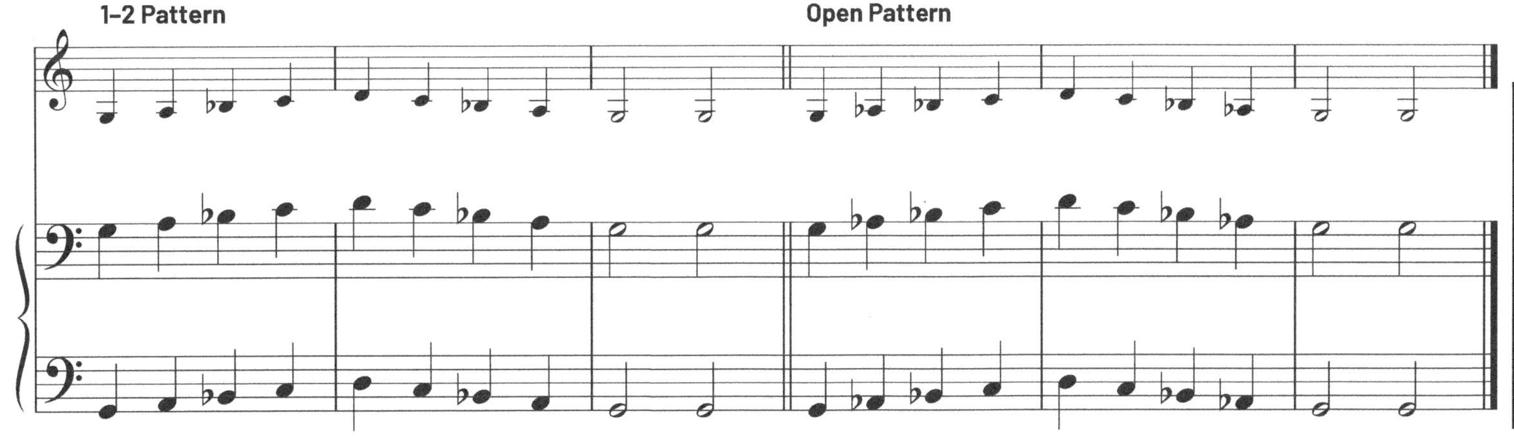

182. C STRING

183. C MAJOR

184. G MAJOR

FINGER PATTERNS

185. D MAJOR

FINGER PATTERNS

186. A MAJOR

FINGER PATTERNS

187. F MAJOR

188. B♭ MAJOR

189. C MAJOR
190. C MAJOR
191. G MAJOR
192. G MAJOR

193. D MAJOR

194. D MAJOR

195. A MAJOR

196. A MAJOR

197. F MAJOR

198. B♭ MAJOR

199. B♭ MAJOR

200. D MINOR (Natural)

201. D MINOR (Natural)

202. G MINOR (Natural)

203. G MINOR (Natural)

204. – *Students improvise melody (line A) to go with accompaniment (line B).*

205. ODE TO JOY (Ludwig van Beethoven (1770–1827) – *Student books have a composition exercise.*

206. PHRASE BUILDERS – *Student books have a composition exercise.*

207. Q. AND A. – *Student books have a composition exercise.*

208. YOU NAME IT: – *Student books have a composition exercise.*

209. TWO AT A TIME

210. ADDING FINGERS

DOUBLE STOPS/FINGERING CHART

Notes

Notes